I CALL BULLSHIT

Also by David Shorr

Bridging the Foreign Policy Divide
(coeditor with Derek Chollet and Tod Lindberg)

Powers and Principles: International
Leadership in a Shrinking World
(coeditor with Michael Schiffer)

I CALL BULLSHIT

Four Fallacies That Keep Our Politics From Being Reality-Based

DAVID SHORR

WONKWORKS

WonkWorks
2509 Peck Street
Stevens Point, WI 54481

ISBN 978-0692770740

Contents

Acknowledgments

By a stroke of terrific luck, the intellectual forerunner of this project was also a source of crucial encouragement and guidance. Not only did the book's central idea come from Thomas Mann and Norman Ornstein's *It's Even Worse Than It ~~Looks~~ Was,* but Norm played a key role in helping me get underway—reviewing the initial concept paper and offering suggestions for how to couch my argument. A number of people kindly reviewed drafts of the chapters on the fallacies. Having spent the bulk of my career in the foreign policy / national security specialist community, I could turn to two of my favorites for help with the "Almighty America" chapter. Heather Hurlburt and Michael Schiffer have for decades disproven the old saw about friends and dogs in Washington. Since I am not as deeply steeped in subject matter of the other chapters, I was that much more dependent on the other reviewers: Jackie Bender, Jared Bernstein, Harold Pollack, and Matt Yglesias. Any weaknesses in the book probably stem from a failure to follow their advice.

Because the chapters on economic, healthcare, and voting rights policy led me into relatively new territory, I also relied on a number of key texts. They are cited in the pages below, but I should list the key authors here: Ari Berman, Ezekiel Emanuel, Jacob Hacker, Richard Hasen, Timothy Jost, Lorraine Minnite, Paul Pierson, and Paul Starr.

I'm grateful to a former colleague, Jill Goldesberry, who helped me figure out several questions of style and consistency. And I appreciated the advice of publishing industry veterans, who were particularly generous given that books are their business: Jim Fetherston, John Oakes, Alex Prud'homme, and Larry Weissman.

Above all I owe more thanks than I could possibly repay to my wife Susan Bender; next it's her turn to take a sabbatical. Finally, I should also say how very proud we both are of our daughter Sadie Bender Shorr as she starts wrestling with how to address the world's problems and injustices.

1

Republicans Need New Material

It's an occupational hazard in my line of work to be ultra-sensitive to the quality and content of debates about public policy. For the past few decades, I have worked for non-governmental organizations whose mission is to affect governmental decisions. All these years as a policy analyst and advocate were bound to shape my outlook, and they ended up stamping me with a certain type of civics-book idealism.

Above all this means putting a high value on the process by which we deliberate over policy choices—and holding that process to a high standard. The marketplace of policy ideas is complex and multi-leveled, but there is no mistaking its importance. For any given issue, the actions of government can be traced back to the tug-and-pull of competing proposals or perspectives. Our system of governance depends on a vigorous competition of ideas just as our economy relies on properly functioning financial markets. In either context, it is essential that the proposals or financial products be offered on the basis of accurate information. For policy discourse, this is the essence of debating an issue *on the merits.*

Likewise, political and financial markets are prone to fail. More to the point, America has experienced both kinds of market failure in recent years. We probably have not yet fully reckoned the causes and consequences of the 2008 financial meltdown. And we have barely started facing the true nature of our dysfunctional politics, particularly the flimflam that Republicans are passing off as policy proposals.

As the GOP has moved farther and farther to the right, it has hammered home a number of simplistic and deceptive notions about the economy, foreign policy, health care, and our elections process. Despite having a very loose relationship to the facts, these ideas have become standard refrains in the public square—treated as one side of the national dialogue. The radicalization of the Republican Party thus raises a very big question for our two-party system: how can America have a constructive discourse about public policy when one of the two major parties has lost its mind?

Now if these sound like the views of a staunch Democratic partisan, they are, and I am. But they have the added virtue of being true. In fact, I could not have imagined undertaking a book like this ten or fifteen years ago—when my work on foreign policy issues was largely apolitical—and I feel provoked into writing it. In earlier times the political split among foreign policy specialists wasn't so sharp, and bipartisan cooperation was much easier. More than anything, this book reflects a personal evolution from my policy wonk roots as I responded to a changing domestic political environment. During the middle part of my career, I stayed out of the partisan political fray and instead got deep into the weeds on subjects like arms control, human rights, conflict resolution, and humanitarian action. As a member of Washington's professional foreign policy community, my job was to help hash out what the U.S. Government should do in response to international challenges. But rarely did those questions become hot-button issues.

Ever since the 9/11 attacks and the Iraq War, though, the spokespersons of Republican foreign policy slid into self-parody. For a brief window toward the end of George W. Bush's presidency, the GOP foreign policy establishment was somewhat chastened by all the ill will stirred by the Iraq War and showed signs of moderating. I know this first-hand because in 2007 I co-led a project that paired up prominent Republican and Democratic policy advisers to find common ground. The resulting book, *Bridging the Foreign Policy Divide*, represented a high water mark for bipartisan cooperation. The Republican contributors included some noted neoconservatives as well as senior Bush Administration officials. All but three of the Democratic participants went on to senior roles in the Obama Administration. One of the sets of co-authors even consulted when one of the pair was working on a foreign policy speech for a top-tier presidential candidate.

Unfortunately, shortly thereafter the GOP reverted to a foreign policy platform that's been as bullheaded as ever. The prevailing conservative stance on every international challenge has been a variation on the same themes: America knows best, the perspectives and interests of other nations don't matter, and American power and insistence can bend everyone else to our will. This compelled people like me to call bullshit on the far-right foreign policy vision / delusion—in order to draw contrasts for the 2008 election, keep policy space open for the Obama Administration once it was in office, and win reelection.

During the 2012 election cycle, I started using one of my blog platforms (Josh Marshall's TPM Café) to address a wider scope of issues and weigh in on domestic and economic policy—feeling, as I say, provoked. To me it was outrageous that the Republicans were campaigning on baseless claims such as the supposed failure of the economic stimulus and government takeover of our healthcare. As time went on, I recognized that the foreign policy fallacy I had been battling was just one in a set of dangerous myths with the same warping effect on our policy debates. What's more, after these fallacies have been pounded into the national consciousness through years of Big Lie-style repetition, they are not going to fade away on their own. All of which helps explain the frustrations for those of us who expected the political pendulum to swing farther to the left after 2008—and the need for this book.

One more personal note related to this project, an unexpected twist right in the middle of the writing process: I became a local politician. Truth be told, my new policymaking role on the City Council of Stevens Point, Wisconsin has more to do with land use and municipal finance than healthcare reform and foreign policy (though employee health insurance does affect the city's budget). Still, the campaign did have a right versus left flavor—since I was challenging an incumbent who was quite skeptical of government's role—and I definitely felt the brunt of Wisconsin's new voter ID law. But mainly, getting more involved in local politics prompted me to weave a string of examples from our state into the book. There was certainly plenty to work with, from Governor Scott Walker's effort to remake our state in the Koch brothers' image, to a duel of op-eds on Obamacare pitting me against a Wisconsin congressman, to the emergence of Janeseville's own Representative Paul Ryan as the new Speaker of the House.

False Premises

In order to get our country's discourse back onto sounder footing, it will require a hard look at the lunacy of the Republican agenda and an insistence that debates on major issues be grounded in reality. We have to make it harder for Republicans to keep saying the same nonsense and getting away with it. We have to force them to come up with new material.

The most vital debates we need are about basic premises. Certain ill-founded ideas hold sway in our politics, policy, and economy based on nothing but the strength of right wing message discipline. Having argued the progressive side of many of these issues on op-ed pages, blogs, or talk radio, I have found the concept of political or policy space to be a good way to explain what is at stake in policy discourse. Whenever opposing sides square off over an issue, their tug-of-war determines the parameters for feasible policy options—the space in which policy makers can maneuver. In raw political terms, the clash of arguments determines who is playing offense and who is back on their heels.

The basic premises for any policy realm are crucial because they define the problem and the terms of debate. They speak to the first-order questions of the political agenda: what items belong on the governmental to-do list and qualify as valid policy objectives? (One of the things they drilled into us in policy wonk graduate school is that senior officials only work on matters that they consider problems in the first place.) Wrapped into the predicates of a policy area are key assumptions about how the world works and the government's instruments for influencing the world.

As indicated by this book's subtitle, I see four false premises as belonging in a special category—the top fallacies with the greatest distorting impact on broad swaths of policy. To name and encapsulate them:

1. Beneficent Job Creators – the private sector elite are the source of all wisdom and prosperity; conversely, the government has a purely negative relationship to the economy.

2. Laissez-faire Healthcare – the best way for Americans to get healthcare is through conservatives' idealized version of a free market.

3. Almighty America – the rest of the world only defies our demands if we let them.

4. Fraudulent Voters – our election results are in danger of being skewed by impostors and others who aren't qualified to vote.

Not that these are the only myths being pushed by the right wing, nor are they the only issues with screwed-up debates. The standard Republican arguments on gun violence, police violence against African-Americans, immigration, and climate change—just to name a few—would certainly never make it through a bullshit detector. So why focus on four fallacies, then, instead of eight or ten?

Of all the BS permeating contemporary American politics, these bogus ideas clog the discussion of large subject areas and haven't been attacked enough to be decisively discredited and begin fading. In other words, far too much of our national conversation is wasted on wildly inaccurate notions of how the economy, health care, foreign policy, and elections really work—misconceptions that are not even debatable. This is what I mean by political market failure. In the marketplace of ideas, truth is supposed to win out over falsehood (with all perspectives having a chance to compete for support). At any rate, we have a lot right wing fantasies being treated as credible Republican counterpoints to Democratic proposals with much stronger roots in reality.

Another reason for leaving climate change off the list of top fallacies is the mounting impatience lately with climate science deniers. In fact, that battle helps illustrate how the truth gains the upper hand and the kinds of victories that can be won along the way. One related fight has been about the most apt language to describe deniers, and whether *denier* itself is a proper label. Debate on how the news media should refer to the denialist faction reached a crescendo, if not a conclusion, in September 2015 when the Associated Press updated its widely used stylebook. As the AP explained, the revision was spurred by an open letter from eminent scientists who protested the use of the term *skeptic*:

> Scientists who consider themselves real skeptics — who debunk mysticism, ESP and other pseudoscience, such as those who are part of the Center for Skeptical Inquiry — complain that non-scientists who reject mainstream climate science have usurped the phrase skeptic. They say they aren't skeptics because "proper skepticism promotes scientific inquiry, critical investigation and the use of reason in examining controversial and extraordinary claims." That group prefers the phrase "climate change deniers" for those who reject accepted global warming data and theory. But those who reject climate science say the phrase denier has the pejorative ring of Holocaust denier so The Associated Press prefers *climate change doubter* or *someone who rejects mainstream science.*

The news agency's proposed solution is avowedly a compromise and has its own problems, as many reactions noted at the time. Has the word *denier* really become so inextricably linked to Holocaust denial? And isn't *doubter* a strange tag for people with such firmly held views? Nonetheless, the AP's move represented a distinct shift in the terms of debate. Deniers are not part of an ongoing scientific inquiry; they are rejecting the conclusions scientists have reached. (As a side note, Wisconsin's first-term Senator Ron Johnson is bucking the trend by taking a climate denial stance as he seeks reelection.)

Another arena in which science rejecters have been

rebuffed is the federal judiciary, where Republican state attorneys general tried to challenge the Environmental Protection Agency's authority to regulate greenhouse gases. The EPA's jurisdiction over carbon emissions is crucial because in the absence of market mechanisms to put a price on carbon (via a tax or cap and trade), regulations will be the main weapons in the U.S. to combat global warming. The litigation also serves an indicator of the right wing's growing credibility problem. After all, getting laughed out of federal court doesn't bode well for their ability to keep resisting scientific consensus.

When you read the U.S. Court of Appeals for the D.C. Circuit's opinion in *Coalition for Responsible Regulation v. EPA*, the judges' exasperation is unmistakable. First there are the opinion's opening lines: "We begin with a brief primer on greenhouse gases. As their name suggests, when released into the atmosphere, these gases act 'like the ceiling of a greenhouse...'" Since their primer is only five sentences long, it seems clear the judges did not consider the science of human-caused climate change to be very complicated.

Indeed some sections of the opinion amount to a dismantlement of the petitioners' arguments about climate science. The court was not impressed, for instance, with the criticism of the EPA for relying on syntheses of scientific findings—as if such analysis is somehow disconnected from the original research. The court's opinion countered that:

> Even individual studies and research papers often synthesize past work in an area and then build upon it. This is how science works. EPA is not required to re-prove the existence of the atom every time it approaches a scientific question.

The judges also called out the attorneys general on another attempt to play scientific arbiters. The court caught the petitioners being highly selective in how they characterized the research compiled by the United Nations' Intergovernmental Panel on Climate Change (IPCC). The opinion noted that the attorneys general "point out that some studies the IPCC referenced in its assessment were not peer-reviewed, but they ignore the fact that the IPCC assessment relied on around 18,000 studies that were peer-reviewed." In essence, the court answered the rejection of mainstream science with variants of the message, 'you are really reaching here.'

The puncturing of climate change denial is both a hopeful and disheartening sign—encouraging because it finally happened, yet troubling that it took so long. There is so much falsehood pervading throughout our politics that commentators have dubbed our era as post-truth or post-policy. One of the great ironies here is that conservatives have benefited from a form of moral relativism. Right-wing fallacies have proven durable because they've undergone so little judgment against objective standards or facts. As much as hard-line conservatives scorn the tendency to look at an issue from all sides—which they portray as squishy—it is that same non-judgmental spirit of openness that's left so much room for Republicans' main arguments about free markets, trickle-down economics, and so-called muscular foreign policy.

It is also a perversion of our two-party system. Under normal circumstances, the credence given to the Republican platform would be perfectly understandable. When a two-party system functions properly, a fair reading of policy debates would recognize valid points on both sides. Such even-handedness becomes a problem, though, if it is applied regardless of substance. It should matter whether or not an argument has a basis in fact, experience, or practicality. A public policy discourse without standards is open to exactly the kind of abuses we have seen from the Republicans. If your arguments are given roughly equal weight as your opponents' no matter the substance of your message, the temptation is to say whatever is politically expedient. In the end, the GOP's most prominent voices have treated the public square as a rhetorical red-light district.

Both Sides Do Not Share Blame

Our dysfunctional politics are a mess of the Republicans' making. Any honest assessment must conclude that the route back to a healthy two-party system is for the Republicans to reverse course after decades of drifting farther and farther to the right. Unfortunately, many of the commentators and reporters who help shape political perceptions take pains to blame the dysfunction and polarization on both parties. But spreading the responsibility requires us to ignore the reality that only the Republican Party has migrated toward the extreme. If anything the Democrats have gotten pulled along somewhat to the right, rather than shifting leftward. Let's not forget, for example, that ideas such as the individual health insurance mandate and cap and trade schemes for carbon emissions were the brainchildren of conservative think tanks.

The more accurate diagnosis is what the scholars Norman Ornstein and Thomas Mann have termed *asymmetric polarization*, and assigning the blame equally doesn't square with the facts. Given how slow the media and the culture have been in recognizing this reality, it was a big deal when the country's two most eminent students of the Congress came out and declared "Republicans are the problem."[1] Unfortunately the trend continued in the four years since, prompting the two scholars to re-title the new edition of their book *It's Even Worse Than It ~~Looks~~ Was*.

As political scientists, Ornstein and Mann offer prescriptions for our system of governance—ways to improve the legislative and electoral processes. Since the present author is a policy wonk and advocate, rather than a social scientist, this book is about the difference between constructive and unproductive discourse. In a healthy two-party system, the center-left and center-right parties hash out the issues between the metaphorical 40-yardlines. As we will see, though, the modern Republican Party is nowhere near the political midfield. Instead of a center-right and a center-left party, we have a far-right and a center party.

The clear trend for Republican policy positions and arguments has been to stand pat on so-called conservative principles—totally rejecting and delegitimizing liberal viewpoints instead of treating them as complementary partners in a creative tension. The overwhelming weight of the conservative argument has tilted toward free-market fundamentalism, utter disdain for government (rarely giving practical parameters for so-called limited government), and a my-way-or-the-highway foreign policy (painting the alternative as appeasement). There simply has been no countervailing trend on the Democratic side of the aisle, nor do mainstream progressive positions tilt so far from the center. Democrats' main policy arguments have stayed connected to the traditional interplay of ideas from the right and left, and they rest more squarely on empirical reality and how the world actually works.

This book's task is to bolster those contentions and show how asymmetric polarization has skewed our national conversation. In chapters on each of the four fallacies, it will expose them as ideologically extreme and impractical. Since the book is focused on basic premises, it will highlight the broad scope of these bogus ideas and the way they distort the issues and options. It's not just that the Republican arguments are wrong, it's that their wrongness has gotten us trapped in silly debates and made it harder to adopt sensible policies. Thankfully, it is still possible to make important strides such as the Affordable Care Act and the Iran nuclear deal. But in the latter case, it took prodigious effort to fend off right wing opposition. Meanwhile all of that acrimony and resistance hinders further progress on the nuclear arms control agenda on urgently needed items such as the Comprehensive Test Ban Treaty—a global taboo against the sort of test explosions that mark a country's arrival as a nuclear-armed power—or further cuts to the US and Russian arsenals.

Since a key claim about the fallacies is that they represent a pronounced shift to the far right, each of the four chapters has a section on historical perspective and the contrast between the extreme ideological Republican positions of today versus the pragmatic moderation of decades past. Sometimes the change has been highlighted when old-school Republicans find themselves at odds with the contemporary GOP, such as former Senator Bob Dole's fruitless push for ratification of the global Convention on the Rights of Persons With Disabilities. In several instances, the history of votes in the Senate offers a longititudinal study of political trends. Who knew that US-Russian arms control agreements, the protection of voting rights, and increases in the minimum wage used to pass the Senate with wide margins of support?

The real touchstones of this book's argument are statements on the issues by prominent Republican political figures—mostly congressional leaders and presidential candidates, but sometimes conservative thought leaders from the commentariat or think tanks. Let me stipulate that the statements might not speak for all Republicans and that there may be intraparty dissension on some issues. For that matter, the 2016 campaign has brought a silly season's worth of BS ideas that are even nuttier than the fallacies. Yet those divisions and affronts aren't as consequential for our national discourse as the consistent message discipline with which Republicans have hammered home the four fallacies (some of them merely extrapolate from the standard party line). Just because blatant racism and xenophobia are considered repugnant by a wide majority, that doesn't make the other baseless pillars of right wing dogma any more plausible or acceptable. Yes, a lot of standard conservative fare looks fairly mild compared to Donald Trump's outrages, but only in comparison to Donald Trump. And is that really where we want to set the bar for one of the two major parties?

The beneficent job creators, laissez-faire healthcare, almighty America, and fraudulent voters will all be familiar to the reader from years of repetition of GOP talking points. From reading this book, you will better understand how they shape our discourse and hold powerful sway over policy options and outcomes. When you run across the fallacies in different political debates, you'll say 'I see what you Republicans did there' and call bullshit on them yourself. If you work in the news media, perhaps you will refuse to accept the talking points at face value and press for stronger arguments and evidence. In other words, this book will have succeeded if it helps make it harder for Republicans to palm off the four fallacies as serious policy arguments and proposals.

The other key set of contrasts, of course, is between Republicans' blinkered far-right ideology and the pragmatic approach of mainstream Democrats. Since we have had a Democratic president for the past eight years, the most prominent expressions of the progressive approach have been President Obama's policies and initiatives. To be sure, no one could claim universal support among Democrats for those policies (though the president's approval rating among Democrats has averaged over 85 percent). Nor can we deny that the Democratic Party has its own internal divisions. The Obama administration's handling of counterterrorism and its use of military force in the Middle East are controversial among progressives. And as we will see, disappointment with Obamacare on the political left has somewhat undermined the president's signature initiative.

Still, there are good reasons to treat the Obama record as a stand-in for the progressive approach to the issues. First of all, far from being political outliers, the president's policies at least represent a considerable weight of opinion among Democrats—as attested by the approval ratings. Second, those policies have been the target of relentless attack from the opposition. Deceptive and baseless as the Republican critiques have largely been, the back and forth between Obama policies and right wing attacks is the substance of recent discourse. Finally, the same goes for the Democrats' internal splits as for the Republicans'; they pale in comparison to the divide between the parties. Progressives' first order of business should be to debunk the right wing nonsense that has cramped the policy space for the progressive agenda.

Those who stubbornly believe in symmetric polarization—who would like to see a plague on both parties' houses—naturally try to spread the blame by pointing to the most liberal Democratic politicians and their policy agendas. There is a crucial difference, though. The Democratic Party's leftmost segment hardly dominates the party in the same way as the far Right rules the GOP. They don't regularly mount and win primary challenges against fellow Democrats. They don't set their party's legislative agenda (it's hard to imagine a Democratic version of voting 60 times to repeal Obamacare). Nor does the Democratic Party's most liberal wing dictate its policy orthodoxy or the catechism of its message.

One prominent theory of GOP intransigence views it as a revulsion toward President Obama personally—mainly in reaction to the country's first black president. There's a lot to be said for the Obama Derangement Syndrome theory, particularly as Republicans choose a nominee who launched his political ascent by questioning the president's birthplace and nationality. But that is not the focus of this project. For one thing, the roots of the fallacies can be traced back long before Obama's election; by now they've simply been pushed to their absurd extreme. Besides, since this is a book about the weaknesses of the fallacies as arguments and policy approaches, it makes sense to dissect them as such, instead of contemplating ulterior motives.

Earlier in the chapter I referred to a creative tension between the conservative and progressive viewpoints, particularly remarking on its absence from today's politics. For the record, the bipartisan in me still yearns for that kind of constructive interchange between the center-left and center-right. Progressivism and conservatism do have complementary insights and concerns to offer. At its healthiest, our two-party system can draw on these approaches and synthesize them into sensible public policy—or at least keep the swings of the political pendulum within a limited range. But again, Republicans must move back toward the center to make such debates possible.

Most of this book highlights the lunacy of conservative ideas that have been taken to extremes, while arguing for more pragmatic liberal alternatives. Republican leaders have staked out such rigid ideological positions that a forced retreat will be a necessary part of the corrective process. So far they have been notably slow in learning the lessons. The 2012 election was widely seen, including by Republicans, as a chance to take the question of Obamacare to the American people—and yet afterward the "repeal Obamacare!" congressional votes kept coming. With that said, though, we can nonetheless imagine what constructive right-left debates might sound like. And so each of the four chapters on the fallacies concludes by suggesting topics and terms on which that set of issues could be argued on their merits.

In all likelihood, our polarized politics will get even uglier before the toxicity starts tapering off. But the first step toward recovery is always to face up to the problem and its source.

Further Reading

Dionne, E.J. *Our Divided Political Heart: The Battle for the American Idea in an Age of Discontent.* New York: Bloomsbury, 2012.

Hacker, Jacob S. and Paul Pierson. *Winner-Take-All Politics: How Washington Made the Rich Richer—And Turned Its Back on the Middle Class.* New York: Simon & Schuster, 2010.

Mann, Thomas E. and Norman J. Ornstein. *It's Even Worse Than It ~~Looks~~ Was: How the American Constitutional System Collided with the New Politics of Extremism.* New York: Basic Books, 2016.

2

Beneficent Job Creators

When I hear Republicans talk about the exalted "job creators" of the American economy, they sound a lot like Colonel Nathan Jessup in "A Few Good Men." According to Republican economic dogma, the job creators provide the rest of America with income and prosperity similar to the way Jessup's Marines take care of our safety and freedom. Both groups are held up as heroes on whom we depend. And in return, the rest of us are supposed to show absolute gratitude and deference.

That is why the Jack Nicholson character comes to mind, particularly his impatience with being questioned about "the manner in which [he] provides" our freedom. But it's Jessup's next line that perfectly expresses the right wing's attitude toward job creators and how we should treat them. Like the colonel, Republicans "would rather [we] just said 'thank you' and went on our way." This isn't to deny the valorous service of marines, soldiers, sailors, or airmen and women, nor the generosity of many business leaders. The problem comes from venerating any group so much that they're off-limits for scrutiny or criticism, paving the way for an abuse of power.

As further proof of how Republicans idolize business executives and put them beyond any reproach, consider the brushback pitch they throw whenever the political debate gets too close for comfort: 'class warfare!' It is their device for trying to shut down any economic policy discussion they don't want to have, at different times aiming it against different policies. It was a top GOP talking point of 2011, used to slam President Obama's push for a major jobs bill to speed the recovery. Then when Mitt Romney was asked about economic inequality during the 2012 campaign, he replied, "You know, I think it's about envy. I think it's about class warfare." Three years later the same charge was leveled at the proposal to increase the minimum wage—traditionally an issue with broad bipartisan support, as we will see.

Such attempts to short-circuit debate are important to bear in mind whenever commentators try blaming both political sides for our dysfunctional politics. Rather than fairly depicting the parties' substantive positions, the idea of equal culpability basically hands the GOP a political victory. The rest of this chapter will show the void at the center of the Republican economic policy agenda—the GOP's fairy tale about business owner heroes, the disconnect with how the economy works in the real world, the resulting distortion of the political debate, and the disastrous supply-side experiments of Republican governors. It concludes, as each chapter does, with sections looking back a few decades to remember a more sensible GOP and peering ahead to sketch the outlines of a healthier right-left foreign policy debate.

Job Creators Good, Government Bad

Naturally Republicans want us to think the Democratic economic program is outright plunder of the wealthy—

which is what Republicans mean when they characterize taxes as the so-called punishment of success. Yet on the question of the roles of the private sector and government, only one party is over at the far end of the spectrum, and it isn't the Democrats. In fact, this is the trick that enables Republicans to use asymmetric polarization to their own advantage: tainting opponents with purported extreme views while pushing a highly ideological agenda of their own.

After all, mainstream progressivism duly credits private enterprise as the engine of economic growth. But it also sees government as a vital complement. Meanwhile, over the past few decades Republicans have been dialing up their rhetoric to the point of delegitimizing, or even demonizing, government. Put it this way, the current Republican position is much closer to pure laissez-faire (including a push to privatize traditional government functions like schools and prisons) than the Democrats are to central planning or the nationalization of private industry. While Democrats make no effort to deny the private sector's integral role, Republicans cast government as an entirely negative factor in the American economy.

The passage below, for example, is from an op-ed in *The Politico* by then-Senate Minority Leader Mitch McConnell on the eve of President Obama's September 2011 address to Congress on his jobs bill. The president, Senator McConnell argued, should admit...

> the failures of an economic agenda that centers on massive government spending and debt. He should then reach across the aisle for a plan that puts people and business at the forefront of any effort to lift the economy...The only way we can bring about a stable, long-term recovery is by shifting the center of gravity away from Washington and toward those who actually create jobs.[1]

Aside from the cheekiness of an opposition leader telling the president to concede failure, the McConnell quote is notable as an illustration of how much weight Republicans give the notion of job creators in their economic platform. According to the GOP, the American economy is utterly reliant on job creators. They are the wellspring from which all meaningful economic activity, employment, and wealth flow. To paraphrase the Gospel of John, nothing comes into our checking accounts except through them.

Once you accept that business interests and a healthy economy are one and the same, it's just a short hop to a policy agenda of simply leaving job creators unfettered to bring the prosperity they are uniquely capable of generating. So in order for America to prosper, we'd better not tax them, regulate them, siphon resources into the public sector, get nosey about the wages they pay, or let unions organize at their places. In terms of government's role, the Republicans argue, the goal is to keep it from being a drag on the economy.

Another opinion piece by a congressmember—this time in local newspapers where I live—showed how these simplistic ideas get stretched to the point of absurdity. In May 2016 Representative Jim Sensenbrenner, who has represented southeastern Wisconsin since the late-1970s, published a hatchet job on the supposed "disaster" of Obamacare. While the next chapter will delve more deeply into healthcare reform, Sensenbrenner's article is worth a glance because of the way it paints the issue as a regulatory burden on employers and ignores the struggles of so many Americans to obtain and/or pay for medical care:

> America's small businesses drive our economy. They employ our citizens, provide vital services, and create products that improve our lives. Yet despite the powerful impact they have on this country, small businesses are struggling under the heavy hand of Big Government. The burdensome

regulations pushed on small businesses [by Obamacare] are the most significant in recent years.[2]

What the congressman offered wasn't a serious argument about policy, but a fable with heroes and villains (which I rebutted in an op-ed for the same newspapers).[3] To make sure no one missed the point, he actually put the name of his story's ogre in capital letters: Big Government. Meanwhile the good guys who own small businesses supposedly provide such benefits to the citizenry it hardly seems right to call them the private sector. Sensenbrenner would have us believe that businesses somehow serve the interests of the public better than government itself. He made them sound so charitable, one wonders whatever happened to the profit motive? But before taking this tale of beleaguered small businesspersons at face value, let's look a bit closer. It is probably safe to assume that this segment of Americans by and large has a household income at or above the $200,000 that would put them in the top five percent. From what we know about wage stagnation and the widening gap between the rich and the rest, Rep. Sensenbrenner is describing the wrong people as struggling.

Then on one of the few points where the congressman referred to substance from the Obamacare debate, he got it wrong. The op-ed mentioned analysis from the Congressional Budget Office (CBO) predicting that the Affordable Care Act would lead to reduced employment. Except the CBO predicted cutbacks the workers themselves would make, not layoffs by employers—a feature of Obamacare rather than a bug. When Obamacare gave workers easier access to insurance (e.g. people with preexisting health problems), they gained new freedom to leave jobs in which they had stayed mainly to hang onto the health benefits. This problem is known as "job lock," and oh by the way, many of those people are going on to start small businesses.

If it seems like all the hosannas for job creators are part of a conscious rhetorical strategy, that's because they are. John Paul Rollert made an empirical study of Republican success in pushing this idea and discovered a sharp spike after President Obama took office. In a search of news media databases, he found 1,082 appearances of the term *job creators* in a single month at the height of the 2011 debt ceiling debate compared with 1,257 references in the entire 48 months of President George W. Bush's second term. As a scholar of Adam Smith, Rollert is also well equipped to spot Republican misconceptions about the free market and chided them for focusing only on capitalism's "visible hand." In other words, the GOP's superficial notion of job creation focuses narrowly on managers' decisions about their workforce while ignoring the underlying dynamic that really drives the hiring process—the market of buyers for the given product or service, which is what Adam Smith actually meant by his term *invisible hand.* [4]

By looking to the great and powerful job creators to give us prosperity, Republicans have reduced economics to a fairy tale and debased the national conversation about the economy. The job creator fallacy sows confusion about the pathology of recessions and their cure. Contrary to what Sen. McConnell said, massive government spending and debt are exactly the right medicine for economic recovery. That was the main lesson from the 1930s Great Depression. In order to make room for the right policies—and recognize that the 2009 $800 billion stimulus package was a success, not a failure—we need an economic agenda with stronger empirical grounding than a fable.

As noted above in the introductory chapter, the 2008 financial meltdown and the dysfunctional state of our politics have both had such sweeping implications that it's a major task simply to reckon them. The former brought the country and the world to the brink of economic cataclysm.

Just by getting close to the edge, the crisis caused enormous hardship for low-income workers and families in the worst position to absorb the blow. For our political system, the test has been to come up with the proper response and learn the right lessons. The combined actions of the Bush and Obama administrations were crucial for the economic recovery, as we will see. The political system, though, was little help. Once Bush left office, near unanimous resistance from congressional Republicans meant that key measures such as the stimulus weren't as aggressive as they should have been. Meanwhile the GOP's worship of job creators grew louder and louder—filling the public square with quackery and making the politics of economic policy a barrier to good policy.

In effect, the presidential elections of 2008 and 2012 served as brackets on the period of meltdown and recovery. Americans went to the polls in November 2008 at almost the exact height of the financial crisis, opting for Barack Obama as a steadier hand to help swing the economy back in the right direction. Four years later things had turned around, but only slowly and partially. To see how politics and conventional wisdom served as hindrances, consider the overarching question of 2012: would it be a referendum or choice election? With the American economy gradually healing from the trauma of the Great Recession, would voters simply judge whether the country was healthy enough, or would they choose between the prescriptions of the two candidates and their parties? From the perspective of a policy wonk, it's a no-brainer. A crude referendum on the national mood would sell our republic short. A truly robust campaign would focus not only on current economic conditions but also the two parties' views about the causes and cure. Surely American voters were able to compare the Obama and Romney platforms on their merits. A hallmark of a functional political marketplace is that good policies are supposed to be good politics. Campaigns should be test beds in which politics sort out the right direction for policy, not political mood rings to gauge how the country is feeling.

The last presidential election provided some reassurance but by no means cured the country's political dysfunctions. Because the pundit and journalist referees of the public square have continued to let right wing fallacies slide—because the mythical job creator is not yet going the way of climate change denial—the next election is once again putting the system to the test. There are still perverse incentives that politically reward bad policies and BS arguments. Returning our discourse to health is an ongoing project. A good place to start rebuilding a reality-based debate is with two business owners who resisted being cast as economic saviors by saying, in effect, 'don't look at me.'

The Customer Really is King

Analysts often use geographic shorthand to refer to the rival camps within the field of academic economics in the United States. The "saltwater" economists on the Atlantic and Pacific coasts see an important governmental role in managing the level of consumer demand in the economy, while "freshwater" economists in the middle of the country put a narrower focus on producers and view government as a distortive force. As it happens, two private sector voices who have offered some of the clearest explanations of the economy are both located in the Pacific Northwest. While their views align with the saltwater approach, we will apply a new label and call them spokespersons for the "Evergreen School" of economics.

Years before helping put his Seattle hometown on course toward a $15/hour minimum wage, billionaire Nick Hanauer published a viral op-ed calling for a heavier federal tax burden on the wealthy in order to "reward true job creators." Hanauer began the essay by sketching his own record of success as an entrepreneur and investor and went on to distinguish that career from the true source of jobs:

> [R]ich people don't create jobs, nor do businesses, large or small. What does lead to more employment is the feedback loop between customers and businesses. And only consumers can set in motion a virtuous cycle that allows companies to survive and thrive and business owners to hire. An ordinary middle-class consumer is far more of a job creator than I ever have been or ever will be.[5]

His point was simple but essential: concentrated wealth doesn't offer a broad enough base for economic growth and prosperity. The interchange between customers and businesses is the lifeblood of an economy, and most wealthy people's resources take the form of investments that also depend on economic activity more than they generate it. As Hanauer explains, he may earn more than the average American by thousands-fold, but he doesn't buy thousands more shirts, shoes, or cars.

Speaking of cars, Hanauer's argument was echoed the co-owner of Hawthorne Auto Clinic of Portland, Oregon. As Congress was debating extension of the Bush era tax cuts, Jim Houser appealed to fellow business owners for help in delivering a like-minded message:

> "The tax cuts for the wealthy won't spur small businesses to hire new workers. That will only happen when our customer base grows—when our nation implements policies that strengthen the economic hand of ordinary Americans."[6]

As our evergreen economists point out, broad-based growth depends on middle- and lower-income households being flush rather than strapped. We need enough people to buy shirts, shoes, cars, and homes so that those purchases spawn further economic activity and jobs. President Obama has made the same point by saying our economy grows "from the middle out, not from the top down."

Conversely, a depressed economy suffers from weak demand—not enough customers for businesses to thrive, leaving them unable to employ workers who would repair cars at Hawthorne Auto Clinic and buy things from other businesses. It's easy to see how the vicious cycle of weak demand feeds on itself in a recession. That is, it would be easy to grasp if not for the misconceptions Republicans have been spreading.

How Wrong Is Republican Economic Reasoning, Let Us Count the Ways

Remember that if it were up to Sen. McConnell and Rep. Sensenbrenner, we would take a cue from Col. Jessup and thank the job creators, with no questions asked. But in order to choose economic policies that really lead to more jobs and prosperity, it is instead crucial that we take stock of the multi-leveled wrongness of the Republicans' ideas. Despite what the right wing says, businesses cannot lead the way out of a recession or meet all of the public's needs. In fact, economic recovery doesn't happen without government spending and debt, which is why President Obama's (and President Bush's) responses to the financial crisis succeeded rather than failed.

Indeed if businesses were the economy's only major players, we would truly be up a creek without a paddle. The government's role in a recession is to make up for the private sector's lack of demand for goods and services. The very nature of the crisis is that consumers and businesses cannot afford to buy anything, a situation that will only get worse if the government stands back and fails to act. In 2008 it was the credit markets that seized up first. When all the bad loans and bonds in the financial markets came to light, suddenly no institutions would extend the short-term credit upon which businesses depend to operate. The economy was grinding to a halt.

Conservatives love to talk about putting the federal government under the same budgetary discipline as private households and businesses. But the government doesn't function the same way in relation to the economy, and it would be disastrous to tighten the U.S. government's belt at the same time the private sector is strapped for cash.

Bringing us now to the point that spurred this book. As part of their critique of far-right GOP ideology, Thomas Mann and Norman Ornstein highlighted multiple problems with the idea of a Constitutional amendment requiring that the federal budget be balanced. One major flaw is that an amendment would take away the fiscal flexibility the federal government needs in order to adjust its budget to a fluctuating economy.[7]

The fact of the matter is that deficit spending—which Republicans always decry as a road to ruin—is actually our economic rescue in a recession. Deficit spending is the mechanism by which the federal government keeps money pumped into the economy to prop up consumer demand (through either increased expenditures, reduced taxes, or both). The real point isn't the similarity between government and households or businesses, it's the contrast. The federal government doesn't face the same danger of bankruptcy as the others and thus is the only economic player with the ability to operate in the red and hang tough until things improve.

Because of this complementarity between the public and private sectors, the guiding principle for the government's fiscal policy is that it should be *countercyclical*. The governmental balance sheet should fluctuate in the opposite direction as the private sector business cycle. The danger comes when the federal government mimics the private sector (also known as *procyclical* policy) by either cutting back in a recession or being profligate in boom times (with the danger of an overheated economy). When John Maynard Keynes was developing his economic principles of demand management in the 1930s, he summed up the countercyclical imperative by saying, "The boom, not the slump, is the right time for austerity at the Treasury."

For my part, I read the Mann-Ornstein critique of the balanced budget amendment proposal and spotted a facet of asymmetric polarization that seemed worthy of special focus. It was one thing for deficit hawks to be so wrong about something so basic. If their ideas were relegated to the eccentric fringe of politics, this wouldn't be much of a problem. The bigger problem is the way their wrongness skews public discussion of economic policy, allowing it to become unmoored from reality.

The "Keynesian Thing"

All of which to say the GOP charge that President Obama's stimulus package failed to bring the country out of the Great Recession is utter nonsense. Senior economists at Princeton University and Moody's Analytics studied the impact of the $800 billion American Recovery and Reinvestment Act (ARRA) approved by Congress within weeks of President Obama taking office (with almost no Republican votes). Calculating how much worse the economy would have been without the ARRA, they credited it with boosting GDP by 3.3 percent in 2010, shaving 1.5 percent off the unemployment rate and saving nearly three million jobs. Take the full set of Bush-Obama policy responses into account—credit facilities to provide liquidity for financial institutions, purchase of their toxic assets, auto industry bailout, and loose monetary policy—and the impact is even more dramatic. Princeton's Alan Blinder and Mark Zandi of Moody's estimated that if the U.S. Government had stood back and done nothing, 17 million jobs would have been lost (twice the actual number), and the unemployment rate would have peaked at 16 percent instead of ten.[8]

As bad as the Great Recession was, it could have been much much worse. From an economic policy standpoint, it stands to reason that the challenge was to stop the freefall and starting to pull the economy back up. (For that matter, the main tool of economics as a discipline is *economic reasoning*, which is the comparison of 'what-ifs' under different scenarios and conditions.) Alas, if only politics were so reasonable and reality-based. In the political arena, conventional wisdom said that average Americans couldn't to see beyond the continuing pain of the recession. Even when political reporters acknowledged that the stimulus fended off a deeper recession, in their next breath they often highlighted the difficulty of making that case to voters. But did that give voters enough credit for being able to dig below the surface?

This uncertainty about the public's grasp of the situation extended to the White House itself, where the president and his team felt quite shaky in their first few years about the case for their reality-based economic stewardship. In Michael Grunwald's definitive account of the ARRA , *The New New Deal*, he follows a prominent thread of internal administration discussions about the challenge of claiming success. At one point Grunwald quotes an impatient Obama telling his advisers, "Look, I get the Keynesian thing. But it's not where the electorate is."[9] Keynes' idea of opening the Treasury Department coffers when the economic slump was pinching household budgets seemed just too counterintuitive to make it stick.

Skeptical about convincing voters that deficit spending leads to more customers for their local auto mechanic, the Obama team was left with somewhat schizophrenic policies and politics. Meeting with other leaders at G20 summits—a forum that was set up for the exact purpose of maximizing growth in the world's major economies—Obama implored

his colleagues not to be overhasty in halting stimulus measures. But at the same time, Obama betrayed the Keynesian
thing by echoing Republican calls for fiscal discipline. While
Obama did add an important caveat distinguishing between
the short- and long-term (putting deficit reduction on the
back end), it was still a unilateral concession to an opposing
party hyping the deficit as the cause of our economic woes.
The truth of the matter was that economic recovery rather
than fiscal discipline / budget cuts was the key to deficit reduction.

Nevertheless, the president's near-term legislative agenda was all about fiscal stimulus. After Democrats lost control
of the House in 2010, the administration's tangles with the
Republican Congressional leadership were chaotic, particularly the summer 2011 standoff over raising the debt ceiling.
There was method to the madness, though. If a follow-on
stimulus package of hundreds of billions wasn't in the cards,
then the president would go for the next best thing and cob-
ble together various bits of stimulus. That is why the deals he
cut with Congress included a temporary reduction of pay-
roll taxes (FICA) by 2 percent, extension of unemployment
benefits, and postponement of budget cuts—anything that
would keep as much money as possible in consumers' hands.
(Another excellent book, David Corn's *Showdown*, gives the
full story of the legislative battles so crucial to the economic
recovery.[10])

Now that the economic and fiscal results are in, the
Democrats were proven right and the Republicans wrong
regarding deficit reduction. The Republicans argued that
cutting the deficit was crucial for the country's economic
health. The facts showed the opposite. Between 2009 and
2015, the budget deficit shrank by more than two-thirds—
from $1.4 trillion to $438 billion—without draconian budget
cuts. In proportion to the economy, the deficit declined by
three-quarters from nearly ten percent of GDP to two and a

half.

Looking back at these political battles, it is hard to put oneself in the shoes of President Obama or his advisers when they shrank from trying to sell the Keynesian thing with the unemployment rate stuck at 9.5 or 10 percent. Even so, recent experience argued for the importance of calling BS on supply-side quackery. One of the truisms of politics is that you can't beat something with nothing. The right wing has built up the job creator myth into a formidable something. It is their story about how the economy works, and they're sticking to it. For President Obama's 2012 reelection and beyond, Democrats have faced an imperative to likewise convey their side of the choice.

And as time went on, and the 2012 election approached, the administration and their allies started doing just that. The most notable instance was the deployment of super surrogate former President Bill Clinton at the Democratic convention, where he offered a forceful rebuttal:

> [W]hen President Barack Obama took office, the economy was in free fall. It had just shrunk 9 full percent of GDP. We were losing 750,000 jobs a month…

> A lot of Americans are still angry and frustrated about this economy. If you look at the numbers, you know employment is growing, banks are beginning to lend again. And in a lot of places, housing prices are even beginning to pick up. But too many people do not feel it yet…

> Listen to me, now. No president — no president, not me, not any of my predecessors, no one could have fully repaired all the damage that he found in just four years.

After the speech, President Obama reportedly said that he should appoint Clinton to his administration as "secretary of explaining shit." Once the campaign season was in full

swing, the candidate himself overcame his reticence and talked about how a thriving middle class was the true source of
prosperity. (At the time I imagined President Obama getting
psyched up by telling himself he'd be damned if Mitt Romney was going to take office and get credit for his economic
recovery.) In the end, even hardboiled political strategists
affirmed that this message was breaking through to the electorate. For instance the following passage from a September
2012 speech by Obama in Woodbridge, VA was pinpointed
by Billy Mann of Penn Schoen Berland as the president's second most effective message of the campaign:

> Top-down economics don't work. This country doesn't
> succeed when only the rich are getting richer. We succeed
> when folks at the top are doing well, but also when the mid-
> dle class is doing well, and folks who are fighting to get into
> the middle are doing well; when more people have a chance
> to get ahead and live up to their God-given potential. [11]

In other versions of Obama's stump speech, that section
also included the line "Our economy does not grow from
the top down; it grows from the middle out." And while the
president didn't talk to voters about countercyclical policy
and demand management, he did sound distinctly like an
Evergreen School economist (Hanauer and Houser would've
been proud) in his discussion of the importance of strong
consumer demand:

> And, look, the whole economy does well when taxes are
> kept low for middle-class families and working families,
> because when you guys have a little extra money in your
> pocket you spend it—you have to—on basic necessities.
> And that means business has more customers and they
> make more profits. They then hire more workers and the
> economy as a whole begins to grow.

Despite concerns about the Keynesian thing being counterintuitive, progressives have a strong case for their economic approach. For one thing, the public actually does grasp that it takes time to bounce back from economic collapse, showing a stoicism that Gallup polls detected all the way through to Obama's second term. From 2010-2013, a steady majority of nearly 70 percent of Americans blamed former President George W. Bush "a great deal" or "moderate amount" for the state of the economy, versus about half for President Obama. So when Bill Clinton told the Democratic Convention that it would've been impossible for any president to fix things in four years, it was a message that resonated beyond the convention hall.

But this is just one of many battlefronts where progressives need to expose the folly of far-right economic ideas. The debate over deficit spending and the need to stimulate consumer demand in a recession addresses only a slice of the pro-job creator agenda. Again, full deference to job creators means freeing them from having to pay taxes, comply with regulations, pay a minimum wage, or deal with unions.

Recall that in Rep. Sensenbrenner's ode to small businesspeople, he gave the private sector credit for meeting a range of public needs and said it was threatened by government's heavy hand. Republicans describe themselves as the party of small or limited government, but their agenda conveys disdain and delegitimization of government. In their unrelenting shift rightward, they have lost all moderation and sense of balance among the different actors and interests in our socio-economic system. The valorizing of job creators has tilted the playing field to the disadvantage of all other players—from wage earners, to organized labor, regulators, educators, and other public servants, indeed leaving little room or role for public service itself.

In the same way that the right wing has misconstrued Adam Smith's concept of the invisible hand, its effort to marginalize government is at odds with the principles of the free market. Contrary to the job creator fallacy, capitalism does not view the marketplace as doing everything better than government does. It actually carves out a major economic category that is supplied exclusively by government. By definition, public goods are those items the private sector simply isn't set up to produce—national highways or armies, city streets, basic research, environmental protection, safety regulations, widely available education, minimum threshold retirement income, or universal healthcare, to name just a few. Some of these things address societal needs, or what is expected in a modern industrialized society. But many of them also are essential for economic prosperity and directly benefit private businesses, as Sen. Elizabeth Warren so powerfully reminded us with her epic "you didn't build that" rant.

For that matter, government plays another vital role in protecting markets from themselves. Regulations not only protect the public from things like pollution and unsafe products, they're also necessary to guard against market failures. Left to their own devices, investors and traders in the financial markets built up levels of risk that eventually blew up in their faces (and in all of ours). That's why the 2010 Dodd-Frank package of financial regulations require banks to keep sufficient assets to offset the risks in their portfolio and have a plan for an orderly wind-down in case the worst should happen.

As already noted, President Obama and congressional Democrats came to the rescue of the American (and world) economy with absolutely critical budgetary stimulus measures—resisted at every step by Republicans who denied government had any ability to create jobs. Meanwhile the GOP also pressed in other policymaking venues to curtail government and clear the way for business interests, often able to carry the day due to legislative majorities and the control of governors' mansions. Inevitably, too, it set up a clash between right wing ideology and practical realities. And sure enough, the Republicans' anti-government program failed to produce the growth and economic bounty they had promised. It turned out that taxes, educators, healthcare, labor protections, and environmental regulations weren't as disposable as the right wing had claimed.

Meanwhile Back in the Lab

In a 1932 Supreme Court dissenting opinion, Justice Louis Brandeis discussed the role of state governments as laboratories of democracy. Given the recent behavior on exhibit by far right Republican legislatures and governors, we now have mad scientists running many of those labs. Just three examples—Governors Sam Brownback of Kansas, Pat McCrory of North Carolina, and Scott Walker of Wisconsin—are reviewed briefly below. A fuller account would need a book of its own to delve Michigan's unsafe drinking water, drug testing of public assistance recipients in Florida, and restrictions on solar panels (but delayed response on fracking-induced earthquakes) in Oklahoma, and other state-level Republican follies.

Voodoo Economics in Kansas

Let us begin with Kansas, where the governor showcased a massive tax cut package as a "real live experiment" in supply-side economics—cuts so huge they appalled pragmatic Republicans and sparked an ultra-rare rebellion within party ranks. In Gov. Sam Brownback's first months in office in 2012, he pushed state income tax cuts through the legislature to the tune of approximately $650 million annually, or approximately 25 percent of Kansas' revenue from income taxes. The hypothesis of this experiment: the effectiveness of tax cuts in spurring private sector growth and consequently generating added revenue.

To be clear, the cuts took effect in 2013 well after the recovery from the Great Recession. In the depths of the recession, the federal government used its fiscal flexibility and deficit spending to help fill gaps in state budgets. Gov. Brownback was actually creating a budget shortfall with the expectation that job creators would, you know, create jobs. To steer this money toward the upper income brackets, Brownback's fiscal policy has been as regressive as possible—reducing taxes of business owners and hiking sales, liquor, and cigarette taxes, which fall heaviest on those with lower income.

Of course the thing about experiments is that they can confirm hypotheses or refute them. Three years later, Kansas ranks sixth from the bottom in economic growth and each new budget report shows a bigger shortfall. And the short-term "fixes" such as diverting highway repair funds, skimping on pension funding, and prematurely collecting tobacco lawsuit settlements (at a discount) will all lead to longer-term problems. On a more optimistic note, primary election victories of moderate Republicans in August 2016 seemed to augur a return to reality-based budgeting in Kansas.

The Governor of ~~North Carolina~~ Duke Energy

In North Carolina, the state's slap-on-the-wrist settlement with Duke Energy over coal ash pollution from two facilities was about to become official when, in February 2014, one of the company's other plants spewed U.S. history's third biggest coal spill into the Dan River. There was no mistaking the intent of the settlement terms, which hit the $20 billion-per-year company with a miniscule $99,000 fine and required only that it study the earlier groundwater pollution rather than cleaning it up. The agreement was right in line with the way North Carolina Republicans have used their newfound power to cater to business interests, but the new coal ash spill inconveniently exposed the speciousness of liberating the job creators for the greater good. Republicans under the leadership of Gov. Pat McCrory, a former longtime Duke Energy executive, pitch their environmental deregulation agenda on the grounds it will benefit the state economically. The reality is much more straightforward: getting the government off the backs of polluters leads to more pollution.

In the two years since the Dan River spill, the legislature and governor have wrangled over the extent of Duke Energy's responsibilities for cleanup. Looking at other deregulatory initiatives that have gone through, you can see how far some Republicans will go in gutting environmental laws and their enforcement. Given the leniency of the earlier coal ash settlement, the changes to North Carolina's law on self-auditing are especially brazen. The law was originally designed to give polluters an incentive to disclose and fix their own compliance failures before being caught by state regulators. Since state governments lack the capacity to regularly inspect all facilities, it makes sense to give companies a chance to find and take care of problems themselves. Under statutes adopted in 2015, though, polluters have the ability to conduct their self-audit even after state authorities find a violation. North Carolina environmental attorney and former regulator Richard Whisnant points out how this changes the incentives:

> The theory of environmental enforcement... has relied on the fact that if you are caught breaking the law, you will have to pay some fine. That threat has been relied on to keep companies honest and on a level playing field. Query whether that theory still works when you can wait for the State to catch you, and if and only if they do, you can fix the problem and get off without any penalty.[12]

As for the state enforcement agency itself, Republicans

have also done their best to reorient it away from enforcement. The agency's new watchword is very much in the spirit of the job creator fallacy. Its political masters have told the agency to focus on "customer service," by which they mean making life easier for North Carolina's corporate citizens rather than working on behalf of the larger number of the state's human citizens.

This same spirit can also be seen in the various measures that curtail transparency and give the public less of a window into companies' environmental impact. And on top of agency budget cuts, the Republicans have brought the staff to heel through a seven-fold increase in positions without civil service protections to insulate them from politics—in effect converting middle managers into the kind of political appointees that serve at the pleasure of the governor.

Dividing and Conquering in Wisconsin

Our governor here in Wisconsin, Scott Walker, is one of the zaniest mad scientists of all. He has done anything and everything possible to clear the way for the job creators and lighten the burden of taxes, wages, and regulations. As Walker has slashed budgets and betrayed long Wisconsin traditions of good government, higher education, labor rights, and environmental stewardship, he's been oblivious to any need for state government to provide public goods. On the other hand, Walker never lost sight of the interests of business owners—even if he sometimes tried hiding the extent to which he was catering to them.

For a number of key issues, the best guide to Governor Walker's agenda has been the items the governor denied supporting. Meet Terry McGowan, president of Local 139 of the International Union of Operating Engineers. His union endorsed Walker's original 2010 election bid as well as his reelection four years later, even after the legislature passed (in the face of mass protests) Walker's infamous law stripping collective bargaining rights from public sector unions such as teachers. Traditionally many private sector unions have enjoyed warm relations with Republican leaders, which McGowan was banking on. More than that, the labor leader took extra steps to confirm Walker's intentions and make sure he wouldn't widen his attack on labor rights to private sector unions. McGowan recounted his 2014 exchange with the governor in a meeting to the *New York Times'* Dan Kaufman:

> "I looked across the table at him and I said, 'we are both god-fearing men. If you can tell me that right-to-work will not come on your desk, then I will take you for your word.' He looked me in the eyes, and he said, 'it will not make it to my desk.'"[13]

Regardless of who Scott Walker fears, he pushed early in his second term for right-to-work legislation that directly targets the dues on which organized labor relies. Nor was this a big surprise, since a hot mic incident emerged in 2012 with Walker divulging his "divide and conquer" strategy to billionaire Diane Hendricks when she asked him about making Wisconsin a right-to-work state.

The University of Wisconsin system has taken a beating from Walker-era austerity, including an attempted revision—which the governor tried denying—of a century-old credo for higher education in the state. In the last biennial budget, the UW system's campuses were forced to make a combined $250 million in cuts. New rules also eased the way for elimination of academic programs and the scholars associated with them. (On our local campus, anthropology was cut from the curriculum.) In other cases even valued faculty members left to take jobs elsewhere, either due to stagnant salaries or the erosion of morale as Republicans have made scapegoats of educators and other public servants.

Yet for all his ideological edge, Scott Walker couldn't publicly defend his administration's attempt to change the Wisconsin Idea, a full-throated argument for the importance of higher education that dates back to 1912. While the Wisconsin Idea links education to the expansion of knowledge as well as civic ideals and public affairs, the Walker administration offered new language emphasizing job skills and workforce development. When the proposed revisions came to light, Walker claimed they were an inadvertent mix-up and referred to them as "drafting errors." Sixteen months and a round of open-records litigation later, though, Walker administration emails indeed revealed a political effort to reorient higher education.

Meanwhile the results have been no better in Wisconsin than in Kansas, North Carolina or any other laboratory. Gov. Walker's policies failed to produce a supply-side miracle and left him with persistent budget gaps. The trick Scott Walker pulled on Terry McGowan has played out on a statewide scale. Walker convinced McGowan that public sector unions could be undermined while private sector unions stayed strong and protected. In the same way, Walker drove a wedge between public sector workers and other voters—stirring up resentment over the tax dollars that go to pay teachers and other employees of state and local government. Through two gubernatorial elections and a recall vote, this divide-and-conquer approach has worked for Scott Walker as a political strategy. But it's been less beneficial to the people of Wisconsin. Attacks on public sector unions go hand-in-hand with the assault on labor rights in the private sector, and stagnant wages are a consequence of both.

To fully appreciate the failure of the Walker experiment, it is instructive to compare Wisconsin to neighboring Minnesota—which has a similarly sized population and economy, but where Democratic Governor Mark Dayton has gone the opposite route of progressive taxation, protection of labor rights, and increases in the minimum wage. The stronger economic performance in Minnesota has received a good deal of attention and coverage, and Ann Markusen delved into the comparison in depth in The American Prospect. Two passages summarize the key indicators:

> Wisconsin suffers from persistently higher unemployment rates than Minnesota, and Minnesota's rate has fallen much faster than Wisconsin's since the beginning of the two governors' terms. From 6.8 percent in January of 2011, Minnesota's unemployment rate fell to 3.7 percent by November of 2014. Wisconsin's initial rate of 7.7 percent fell to 5.2 percent in the same period. Slower job growth and higher unemployment rates have encouraged net out-migration from Wisconsin.
>
> ...
>
> After four years of diverging labor policy regimes, Minnesota's wages are both higher and have increased modestly faster. In 2013, Minnesota average annual wages were $47,370, up 4.2 percent from 2010. Wisconsin's gains were more modest, with the annual average wage of $42,310, up 3.4 percent. Minnesota's better wage rates are largely responsible for superior household incomes. From 2010 through 2013, Minnesota's median household income jumped from $52,300 to $60,900, a growth rate of 16.4 percent, while Wisconsin's comparable median moved from $50,400 to $55,300, expanding 9.7 percent.[14]

And of course Minnesota is maintaining its investments in education, and by extension a well-prepared citizenry and workforce.

Next we will look back at some of the Republicans' previous policies, before they were mad scientists. If the GOP truly is radically right of center in a way it didn't used to be, it helps to have a before-and-after picture of their agenda. We will make the comparison in three ways. First, we'll focus on how Republicans handled the Keynesian thing. Did they support reality-based countercyclical policies and help provide economic stimulus during recessions? Next we will examine the voting record in the U.S. Senate on the federal minimum wage as a longitudinal study of an issue on which today's Democrats and Republicans are sharply split. Third will be a look at earlier Republican views on the roles of the private and public sectors, before this chapter's final section on what a more constructive right-left debate might look like.

They Were All Keynesians

In 2011 I had a speaking gig at a small Midwestern college and spent the afternoon getting to know my host, the leader of the local World Affairs Council. At one point he described himself as a conservative Republican and, based on a hunch, I gave him a one-question quiz on fiscal policy. "Why has the budget deficit spiked up?" I asked. My host answered that the recession had depressed revenue while also increasing expenditure on social safety nets like unemployment benefits and food stamps. This confirmed my hunch. He was absolutely correct on the substance and dead wrong in where he placed himself on the political spectrum. His answer about the natural consequences of a recession was too reality-based for today's Republican Party, which views the deficit as the byproduct of President Obama's socialistic radical expansion of government. My host was like an old-fashioned conservative preserved in amber. He showed that conservatives haven't always been fire-breathers who rail against government as the enemy of freedom and capitalism.

What is the history of Republican economic policy during recessions? Have they always believed in the quackery of austerity? Looking at the most recent Republican president, one of George W. Bush's most revealing moments as a closet Keynesian was also an episode that has drawn harsh criticism from liberals. In his handling of the September 11 attacks, President Bush is often slammed for squandering a moment of national and international unity. And there is no question that his decision to invade Iraq—a country that had nothing to do with the attacks—was a scandal of historic proportions. But his impulse to encourage Americans to go on living normal lives doesn't deserve the ridicule it has drawn from critics who lambaste Bush for telling us to go shopping (words he didn't actually use).

Even just as a response to terrorism, this approach of not letting ourselves be terrorized is much more sensible than the Bush team's subsequent threat-hyping and fear-mongering. But as a matter of economic policy it was also a departure from the job creator fallacy, acknowledging the American economy's reliance on strong consumer demand. Similarly it's worth remembering the post-9/11 message of "America's Mayor" Rudy Giuliani, who implored everyone to "Come to New York. Spend money." (Personally I remember in September 2001 going back to New York, where I grew up, and being approached by numerous of out-of-towners to ask for directions, including a first-time visitor from Israel who made a point of telling me he brought money to spend.) The rescue package President Bush approved for cash-strapped airlines was an even more tangible Keynesian intervention.

To summarize the record of Republican presidents during recessions, they generally avoided Herbert Hoover's disastrous example while also stopping short of full-on Keynesianism. From the Great Depression to the Great Recession, for instance, the worst downturn was in the first two years of Ronald Reagan's presidency. The Reagan Administration's stated, and attempted, policy was to rein in spending and taxes. Whatever their supply-side intentions, President Reagan recoiled from the most difficult budgetary choices—protecting not only his military buildup but also some domestic spending and loophole tax expenditures—and ultimately responded to the recession with countercyclical deficit spending.

Unlike Reagan, George W. Bush purposely resorted to economic stimulus for the recessions at the beginning and end of his presidency. Even so, he kept some plausible deniability by putting the bulk of his stimulus in the form of tax cuts (the Obama ARRA stimulus package involved a greater mixture of both spending and tax cuts). From a Keynesian perspective, spending increases and tax cuts both stimulate a depressed economy because in either case the government keeps money flowing while the private sector is faltering. The right wing's laissez-faire absolutists argue that regardless of boom or bust, leave money in the taxpayers' own pockets—particularly in the pockets of the investor/owner class—and cut government down to the smallest possible size. So where does that leave Bush's penchant for tax-cutting, in times of feast and famine alike, and his ballooning budget deficits due to a failure to cut spending? The tilt of the Bush tax cuts toward the wealthy were certainly in the spirit of a supply-sider, but the budget deficits in the economic boom times of the mid-2000s put him on the wrong side of both camps. The high spending, much of it driven by the wars on terror and in Iraq and Afghanistan, is the basis for criticism of Bush within his own party for being a big government Republican. During the seven full fiscal years Bush was in office, the federal budget grew from two to three trillion dollars with an average deficit of $269 billion. This also ran afoul of demand-side economics (aka economics) because the government should be running a surplus when the economy is performing well. Compare this with President Bill Clinton, whose final four budgets had an average surplus of $140 billion.

When the mortgage-backed securities hit the fan in 2008, though, the Keynesian Bush did everything short of New Deal-style programs to counter the collapse of the financial markets. For the financial industry itself, the Bush team worked to avert a total meltdown by bailing out Fannie Mae, Freddie Mac, and AIG and taking the sketchiest holdings off investment banks' balance sheets via the Troubled Assets Relief Program. The auto industry rescue was also initiated under Bush, though it was completed under President Obama. Meanwhile President Bush's last round of tax cuts in 2008 was an explicitly Keynesian stimulus (mainly in the form of millions of $600 checks mailed to American households).

So when you look back at the last several decades, President Obama's Republican foes in Congress were the only national GOP policymakers zealous enough to push austerity in a weak economy. In fact, even the party's 2012 nominee for president had moments of sounding suspiciously Keynesian. Early in that election year, Mitt Romney warned of the danger of austerity: "If you just cut, if all you're thinking about doing is cutting spending, as you cut spending you'll slow down the economy."

The Stagnating Federal Minimum Wage

The famous Harry Truman epithet about the "do-nothing Congress" of 1948 not only fits the Republican-dominated Capitol Hill of today, it holds a special irony. As it happens, one of the few measures President Truman managed to push through was the first federal minimum wage increase since the enactment of the Fair Labor Standards Act just over a decade prior. As of this writing, Congress has gone more than nine years without raising the minimum wage (currently $7.25/hr) due to Republican intransigence. To put this in perspective, in the last 55 years there has only been one longer stretch of time without the enactment of a minimum wage law: 1977-1989.

In other words, before Congressional Republicans were sworn to resist the minimum wage as a job-killing liberal ideological plot, it was something they voted for roughly every 4-7 years. Looking at the last four Senate votes on the minimum wage, it's interesting to see just how much Republican support it enjoyed. The two most recent instances—in 2000 and 2007—drew minimal opposition of two and three votes respectively. But when legislation like this draws such overwhelming Republican support, it's usually because of other sweeteners in the legislative package that tilt their way. So it is more instructive to look at results from the preceding two minimum wage hikes, which weren't as less lopsided; the intra-Republican split in favor of an increase in 1989 was 36-8 and 31-22 in 1996.

For another contrast between past and present Republican positions, let's turn once again to Sen. Mitch McConnell. When the 2007 legislation passed, then-Minority Leader McConnell was filled with the spirit of bipartisanship:

> This is a testament to what we can accomplish when we work together to move critical legislation forward...We look forward to working with the House of Representatives to send a final bill to the President that will be a victory for both those who earn the minimum wage and those who pay it.

Yet McConnell took a very different tone seven years later, during mid-term elections that would ultimately promote him to the job of majority leader. In 2014 he was caught on tape at a Koch brothers-hosted conference promising to keep the Senate from voting on the minimum wage.[15]

To a large extent, the radical anti-government Republican Party of today is the creation of Charles and David Koch. They were libertarians before it was cool and steadily built up the ideological platform, consistent messaging, base of activists and donors, and cadre of politicians we now see. The result is a party confined to a small tent and a very narrow range of opinions. When staunch conservatives such as former Utah Sen. Bob Bennett and former House Majority Leader Eric Cantor were defeated in primaries by fellow Republicans attacking them from the right, it shattered any illusion of pluralism or pragmatic forces within the party. Republican leaders in the House of Representatives struggle to keep their Freedom Caucus colleagues from completely bogging down the necessary business of governing, but it is clear who has set the limits on the GOP agenda. When avoiding government shutdowns or defaults on the national debt count as victories, and Paul Ryan serves as a moderating influence, your party has gone pretty far down the far-right rabbit hole.

Against that backdrop, Jacob Hacker and Paul Pierson have done a valuable service in retracing the evolution of conservatism and the GOP and remembering what they stood for before ideological inbreeding cut them off from practical reality. At a time when valorization of the private sector has given the job creators free rein, Hacker and Pierson's recent book *American Amnesia* documents the balance of complementary forces that used to be valued by the country's leaders—even its business leaders. In our amnesia we have forgotten the essentials of our own success: a mixed economy with a vital role for the public sector and a prosperous working class that was protected and sustained by organized labor.

One of the book's most interesting chapters focuses on corporate leaders from the post-War period who were the mirror image of the Koch brothers. In the recent years now that it's no longer taboo to debate economic inequality (thank you, Occupy Wall Street), many of us have begun remembering the broadly shared prosperity of the 1940s-1970s. Hacker and Pierson further remind us that a major segment of corporate America were very much with the program of broad-based growth. For instance they unearthed the history of the

Committee for Economic Development (CED), a powerful network of business executives promoting ideas that would be anathema to today's corporate lobbies. Because they believed in the importance of labor unions, CED opposed efforts by the contemporary version of the Koch brothers—which probably included Koch Industries patriarch Fred Koch—to repeal the Wagner Act that protects organized labor rights. The quotations Hacker and Pierson found from CED co-founder Paul Hoffman of Studebaker are remarkable:

> "The major emphasis which capitalism places on the individual does not preclude collective activity. As a matter of fact, the interests of the individual can be advanced only through a wide range of collective actions, both governmental and private."
>
> and
>
> "The emerging CED attitude has been that 'government has a positive and permanent role in achieving the common objectives of high employment and production and high and rising standards of living for people in all walks of life'....The greatest single achievement of CED...may turn out to be the clarification it has been developing on the role of government in the economy."[16]

How nice it must have been to have corporate opinion leaders in that part of the political spectrum. Indeed it makes you wonder about the possibility of reviving that center-right perspective.

All Mod Cons

You wouldn't know it from listening to Republican politicians, but there actually is a cadre of moderate conservative policy wonks with proposals for how to pull the GOP toward the center. For many of them, the reformist project is about offering policies to ease the stresses and strains weighing heavily on so many American households. And unlike the immoderate conservatives who dominate the party, they harbor no illusions that problems like unemployment and stagnant wages will be fixed by benevolent business owners or the miracles of tax cuts and free markets. The so-called reformicons recognize the disconnect between standard Republicans' bromides and the difficulty many Americans face in making ends meet. Instead of viewing social insurance programs with suspicion—focused more on supposed cheaters than demonstrable genuine needs—the reformists have launched a discourse on innovations to update them.

At an October 2013 conference hosted by former Gov. Jeb Bush, American Enterprise Institute (AEI) President Arthur Brooks gave a stern rebuke to fellow conservatives for their attack on federal anti-hunger programs:

> One of the things, in my view, that we get wrong in the free enterprise movement is this war against the social safety net, which is just insane. The government social safety net for the truly indigent is one of the greatest achievements of our society. And we somehow want to zero out food stamps or something, it's nuts to want to be doing something like that. We have to declare peace on the safety net.[17]

Without citing him by name, Brooks may have been taking aim at Speaker of the House Paul Ryan, who enjoys an inside-the-Beltway reputation as a serious policy wonk but whose budget proposals consistently call for weakening the safety net.

Meanwhile one of Brooks' AEI colleagues, Michael Strain, stands out among reformicons as an avatar of reasonableness. Strain published a detailed, substantive look at the problems of the labor market in *National Affairs* entitled "A Jobs Agenda for the Right." Unlike many movement conservatives in the GOP who claim their party is center-right, Strain's article could justifiably be labeled an agenda for the center-right. For example, Strain gives a very different take on the mismatch between the skills workers possess versus those that are in-demand from employers. Typically Republicans discuss this question in blame-the-victim terms that put the onus on workers to develop the right skills, yet Strain looks at it from the standpoint of geography. The same industry that may be faltering in the region where a worker currently lives often is thriving in another area. Therefore Strain proposes measures to help workers identify those opportunities and subsidize relocation, which could be well suited to a society as mobile as ours. He also called for unemployment insurance benefits to be paid in larger monthly chunks rather than being parceled out weekly.

And in another act of supply-side heresy, Strain endorsed the role of the Federal Reserve's monetary policy in helping create jobs and welcomed the Fed's dual mandate to keep both inflation and unemployment low. This dovish stance on inflation is a refreshing break from the far-right's relentless hyping of the inflation threat and demonization of the central bank. After all, in the depths of the Great Recession the Fed's stimulus tripled the money supply without setting off an inflationary spiral.

What's most intriguing from the standpoint of the potential for bipartisan compromise are Strain's ideas about prioritizing public investment:

> Jobless recoveries suggest a particular fiscal-policy response: Instead of short-term stimulus as a countermeasure to recession, policy should focus on longer-lived investment projects. The projects selected should have high social value—they should involve things we would want to do even in the absence of a demand shortfall.[18]

This points to a potentially fruitful policy debate that steers federal budget resources toward the kind of public goods that will help sustain the American economy's growth and productivity. Even more broadly, the country and the economy would be well served if experts from the center-right and center-left could join forces to find the best answers for economic growth and employment. Remember, the danger of the far right's fallacies is their distortion of basic premises and realities, leading the GOP to define policy problems bizarrely (e.g. liberating employers to pay the lowest wages they can). If moderate conservatives and progressives could reach common definitions of the problems, the economic policy debate would be much more constructive.

Not So Fast, With the Bipartisanship

But we should be careful not to mistake a crack in the doorway for a significant political opening. The political problem is akin to the economic one; the mess we are in was a long time in the making, and we won't get out of it overnight. The Washington Post columnist EJ Dionne has been a close observer of GOP's rightward drift as well as the efforts of the reformicons. Writing about the reformicons' proposals and ideas for the journal *Democracy*, Dionne voiced doubts that the reformists represent a powerful new force. He also poses a useful test of their seriousness: "To the extent that reform conservatives are willing to battle the Tea Party's reflexive hostility to government, they will be part of the solution."[19] As with so many things, the first crucial step is to squarely face the problem.

With his call for fellow conservatives to celebrate the social safety net instead of attacking it, Arthur Brooks' certainly seemed to gird himself for battle. And yet we have other statements from the AEI president that shrink from the fight. In May 2015, EJ Dionne hosted a panel discussion at

Georgetown University on combating poverty with Brooks and President Obama as the panelists. On that day, Brooks offered very different peace terms:

> Look, no good economist, no self-respecting person who understands anything about economics denies that there are public goods. There just are public goods. We need public goods. Markets fail sometimes—there's a role for the state. There are no radical libertarians up here, libertarians who believe that the state should not exist, for example. Even the libertarians don't think that. So we shouldn't caricature the views of others because, in point of fact, that impugns the motives.

The president, though, didn't consider the idea of conservatives minimizing government's role to be a caricature—and rightly so. President Obama countered Brooks by reporting that when he has talked to conservatives in private settings (as opposed to panel discussions), they sound more like Ayn Rand than Brooks lets on. But the denial of public goods has been even more public and blatant than that. How else to explain Congress' slowness in passing a transportation bill—given that roads and infrastructure are classic and widely recognized forms of public goods? Then there were the refusals by Wisconsin Governor Scott Walker and New Jersey Governor Chris Christie, with great fanfare, to accept federal funding to update the railways and tunnels in their states.

Even as he makes the case for reform, Arthur Brooks sometimes slips into shopworn slams against the public sector. In his reform manifesto "Be Open-Handed Toward Your Brothers" in *Commentary*, he decries the growth in spending on education as a windfall that has enriched the people who work in that field.[20] Not to deny the issue of teacher accountability—my family and I have had our own run-in with the public schools—but this is an odd moment to demonize teachers. When the Great Recession eviscerated state and local tax revenues, teachers were among the most vulnerable professions in the country. A special fund in the stimulus bill prevented 300,000 teachers from being laid off, about half the expected layoffs and effectively a 5.5 percent federal subsidy of the entire national K-12 system.[21] Is reducing education budgets and workforces really a key plank in the education reform platform? At any rate, it hardly seems part of a non-libertarian, of-course-there-are-public-goods agenda.

Of course the real test of reform-minded moderate conservatism will be whether its ideas move from policy journals to policy decisions. As with the rail and tunnel funds, Republican governors have faced another important test of their belief in public goods and the social safety net: expansion of Medicaid at the state level under Obamacare. It is an issue on which Governors Walker and Christie split, and it's the subject of the next chapter.

Further Reading

Corn, David. *Showdown.* New York: William Morrow, 2012.

Grunwald, Michael. *The New New Deal.* New York: Simon and Schuster, 2012.

Hacker, Jacob S. and Paul Pierson. *American Amnesia: How the War On Government Led Us to Forget What Made America Prosper.* New York: Simon & Schuster, 2016.

Krugman, Paul. *End This Depression Now!* New York: W.W. Norton, 2012.

3

Laissez-faire Healthcare

Republican rhetoric sends mixed messages about health-care consumers. On the one hand, the right wing wants to empower consumers so we have more choices and can take charge of our own health. But conservatives also talk about the importance of consumers having skin in the game so that we don't grab too much free stuff from the healthcare system, which is a much less empowering sentiment. Naturally Republicans fret about the government coming between you and your doctor—even crying 'government takeover!' against reforms that are based on private insurance—though they seem less concerned about those of us who don't have a doctor.

The underlying fallacy of the Republicans' argument is the way they look at modern medicine as if it's a trip to the supermarket. Republicans' free market fundamentalism is impractical generally, but healthcare is a particularly bad testing ground for laissez-faire ideology. As we know from common sense and experience, obtaining healthcare is not a typical purchase of a good or service. Instead it is a mixture of risk management and putting trust in experts more knowledgeable than ourselves.

The platonic ideal of the marketplace simply doesn't jibe with the healthcare realities we face. When you really think about it, the notion of responsiveness to consumer needs isn't very useful in describing the problem. When I seek diagnosis or treatment of my health, I don't consider myself as being on the 'buy side.' A visit to the doctor is not an assertion of purchasing power. It isn't my consumer preference that leads me to the doctor's office; I go because I need the advice and help of medical experts. Rather than judging the healthcare provider, I am seeking out their professional judgment on my health. So there is a built-in contradiction in the conservative argument. While Republicans guard vigilantly against the governmental interference in the sacred trust between doctor and patient, their proposals expect the patient to keep the doctor at arm's length and play the role of finicky customer. The writer and physician Atul Gawande mulled this idea during an interview with a Texas heart surgeon for his article on "The Cost Conundrum" for *The New Yorker.*

> We tried to imagine the scenario. A cardiologist tells an elderly woman that she needs bypass surgery and has Dr. Dyke see her. They discuss the blockages in her heart, the operation, the risks. And now they're supposed to haggle over the price as if he were selling a rug in a souk?[1]

Nor is the purchase of medical care a typical item in the household budget. An individual or a family's future healthcare needs are a roll of the dice—liable to spike dramatically at any moment due to traumatic injury, heredity, or pure happenstance. And it is the price tag associated with those spikes that exposes the average American household to such financial insecurity and distress. Those who are in the lowest income brackets can't afford basic medical care, while the cost of treating major illness or injury threaten middle class Americans with financial ruin. How do you budget for medical expenses that run into the tens or hundreds of thousands? Remember, medical bills were the leading cause of personal bankruptcy before Obamacare went into effect.

Fortunately there's this thing that helps deal with the uncertainty and risk of large unanticipated expenses. It's called insurance, and here's how it works. The basic business model is to take in enough money in premiums from a large group to pay for the subset of customers who need to collect claims on their coverage. Insurance sets up pools of customers who all confront certain kinds of hazards and then spreads the risk so that everyone pays a little and the money is there for the unlucky few. Now what is the point in going over rudiments of insurance and risk management that you probably already understood? Because it helps expose the problems in the right wing approach to healthcare reform.

But before getting too deeply into Republican proposals on health insurance, we should pause to note how conservatives leave insurance out of the picture for some elements of their approach. To the extent possible, Republicans want to create free markets for the provision of healthcare itself rather than health insurance. The aim of health savings accounts and related tax credits is, once again, to give people the skin in the game and empowerment to be discriminating consumers. By channeling healthcare dollars into households, Republicans would like to make us—and not insurance companies or programs—the purchasers of medical care. One danger of having consumers hold tightly to their healthcare dollars, however, is when they forgo care they actually need. If consumers are too tight-fisted, they can get into more serious health (and healthcare cost) problems by avoiding the doctor or the treatments physicians have recommended for them.

Republicans define the healthcare reform problem differently. The doctor-patient relationship and risk of six-figure medical bills are not their main concerns. Mostly they want a free exchange of medical products and services so that healthcare functions efficiently and the market is left to sort things out. Republicans have put their romanticized idea of individual free choice above all else, even though it isn't appropriate in all contexts.

As discussed in the last chapter, markets are prone to failure, and we need government to set up regulatory frameworks that keep market forces from spinning out of control. In the financial markets, it was a buildup of risk and leverage combined with proliferating derivatives contracts that were turning Wall Street into a gambling parlor. In healthcare, it was ever-mounting costs that, if unchecked, would leave little room for anything else. The 17 percent of GDP spent on healthcare in the early-2010s represents a doubling of the percentage in the late-1970s. Before Obamacare was passed, estimates were that healthcare spending would be 28 percent of our economy by 2030 and 34 percent by 2040 (fortunately the proportion has stabilized at around 17 percent since enactment of the ACA).

In short, leaving healthcare to the magic of the market was not working and would not be sustainable for household or government budgets. Given what we know about wage stagnation, rising insurance premiums have been a big factor in depressing wages—with employers tilting their employees' compensation packages toward benefits instead of wages. This is can be a double whammy for workers saddled with increased shares of premiums, copayments, and deductibles, but less income to pay for them. The federal and state budgets also faced a similar squeeze; more spending on healthcare means fewer resources for K-12, higher education, or transportation. In other words, even if Republicans didn't view the large number of uninsured Americans as a compelling problem in itself—and 20 million Americans now have coverage thanks to Obamacare—the runaway train of healthcare cost growth should have gotten their attention. Unfortunately the pulls of ideology and party discipline have been just too strong.

Vice President Joe Biden famously said it was a "big fucking deal" when Congress passed the ACA. Yet it was also a big deal that the other major political party refused to engage constructively and have a hand in the largest set of healthcare reforms in four and a half decades—particularly given the ominous cost growth trends mentioned above. This is the depth of political dysfunction with which we still need to reckon. For all the times President Obama has taken heat for failing to reach across the aisle, there must have been amnesia about the healthcare reform push. Given the total Republican boycott of support for the Obamacare bill, the 2009 talks with GOP interlocutors in Congress hardly seem in good faith. Not that there is any great mystery here, Republican congressional leaders made clear their insistence on a unified front. By their calculation, being unanimously opposed would enable Republicans to slam the ACA in the most apocalyptic terms (including for its lack of bipartisanship).

In terms of substance, the strategy of total obstruction only compounded the Republicans' problems. The rest of this chapter will highlight the contradictions, deceptions, and misconceptions of the GOP healthcare argument. It will show the problems of their attempt to cherry pick Obamacare's popular provisions and the trap that makes them unable to put forward a workable alternative. We will home in on the true objective of the GOP's position and how it connects to President Obama's famous promise that "if you like your insurance, keep your insurance." You will also meet a Central Wisconsin Republican—just down the road from me—whose view of the president and the ACA changed radically after Obamacare saved his life. The chapter's last few sections will look back at the reform proposals yesteryears' moderate Republicans as well as the moment of decisive break with common sense (spoiler alert: it involves Bill Kristol), then look ahead at the prospects for bipartisanship.

According to the right wing, the biggest horror of health care reform is the individual mandate requiring everyone to have insurance—despite the proposal having originated within their own conservative circles. The instant that the mandate became part of Obamacare, Republicans became staunch defenders of the fundamental freedom to not buy something. As they see it, the requirement to obtain insurance was a fast track to tyranny, foreshadowing even darker days when Americans will be forced to buy broccoli. In a free market, why should the government have the power to dictate which products consumers will or won't buy? Shouldn't healthier people be allowed to buy just the medical treatment they need, instead of paying expensive monthly premiums?

Unfortunately this argument is at odds with the essence of insurance and the very nature of a risk pool. And it's a departure from Republicans' usual deference to the private sector. In a nutshell, any company that has mostly high-risk customers with health problems and fewer low-risk customers won't be profitable unless they charge their less healthy customers exorbitant premiums. It is precisely because the American healthcare system gives such a large role to private insurance companies—rather than actually being taken over by the government—that the individual mandate is necessary. When the insurance industry helped craft Obamacare's grand bargain, gaining additional healthy customers via the individual mandate was the sine qua non for them to be more generous toward the unhealthy (coverage for preconditions, lifting annual and lifetime caps, etc).

The basic flaw in the Republican approach is a misguided individualism that views each household in isolation.

They fail to recognize that when it comes to healthcare, no man or woman is an island. Along with their opposition to the individual mandate, Republicans emphasize Americans' freedom to purchase as little coverage as they want. As will be obvious from their proposals, the GOP healthcare platform isn't about extending health coverage to those who lack or need it. Instead their agenda focuses on insulating those with less need for healthcare.

This is a very blinkered way to look at the issue. For one thing, the healthy don't necessarily stay that way. An insurance plan might look like a great deal until you really need it, and the deductibles, copayments, and caps limiting the insurer's outlays all kick in with a vengeance. And as mentioned above, without a proper risk pool, those with the greatest medical needs are left with crushing costs.

"Neat, Plausible, and Wrong"

In December 2015 Representative Paul Ryan outlined his agenda as the new Speaker of the House in a major speech at the Library of Congress. As we know, the House Republican majority that Speaker Ryan now leads has a fetish for voting to repeal Obamacare. For his part, Ryan has built a reputation in Washington as a wonkish policy intellectual and disciple of Ayn Rand. The synopsis of the healthcare reform debate in Ryan's Library of Congress speech is worth noting:

> The other side thinks that to lower costs for some people you have to raise them for others. Life is a zero-sum game. They know people won't buy pricey insurance. So their solution is, don't give them a choice. We say lower costs for everybody by giving them that choice. Instead of forcing you to buy insurance, we should force insurance companies to compete for your business. Let people find a plan that works for them.

And when Speaker Ryan says "force insurance companies," he of course means not force insurance companies to do anything. Above all this agenda is about deregulation. It is predicated on empowered consumers exerting the same market pressure on health insurance that Republicans envision for medical care itself. It also raises similar questions about the purported power of consumers. Does deregulation really put us in a position to get the best possible deal? Do the new rules under Obamacare somehow hinder insurance companies from offering me a better value on my coverage?

A century ago the great American philosopher and curmudgeon HL Mencken seemed to anticipate today's Republicans with his classic observation that "there is always a well-known solution to every human problem—neat, plausible, and wrong." The marketplace doesn't offer a real solution to the high cost of health coverage. Unrestrained competition can help give us cheaper computers and smart phones, but it isn't much use in the fight against medical inflation. Computer manufacturers offer consumers a better value by lowering the cost of producing a computer. Insurance companies, meanwhile, are medical bill-payers rather than providers of care. They don't have the same degree of control over the process as a manufacturer, and as we saw in the pre-Obamacare world, they were losing the battle to contain costs.

Faced with rising costs, insurance companies keep their premiums affordable mainly by skimping on coverage. While it's nice to imagine empowered consumers squeezing a better deal out of insurers, the more likely scenario is a familiar one: health plans that limit the insurer's payout and put a greater burden on the policy holder. Naturally you can get a great deal on a policy that excludes pre-existing conditions, makes the customer responsible for substantial deductibles and co-payments, and limits the total that the insurer would have to pay annually and cumulatively. But then, that isn't a very good deal.

And regardless of what Paul Ryan says, it is impossible to avoid zero-sum trade-offs in health insurance. Again, this is inherent both in the risk pools necessary for any insurance as well as Obamacare's grand bargain with the industry. In order to cut prices for some people, you do have to increase them for others. To keep people with medical needs from being crushed by healthcare costs, it requires that healthier people chip in more. In order to cover preexisting conditions and get rid of annual and lifetime coverage caps, insurance companies need an individual mandate to broaden their customer base.

All too often, Republicans seem to view America as a loose collection of individuals rather than a society. In healthcare reform and other spheres of policy, they have a large blind spot that keeps them from seeing the ways in which we are all inevitably interconnected and the challenges that can only be tackled collectively. This issue reminds me of people who complain about being forced to pay property taxes even though they don't have kids in the public schools. Econ 101 teaches us about public goods as a category of things that the marketplace won't produce and therefore depend upon government acting on behalf of society as a whole. In other words, we can't have an educated populace or universal healthcare if people are allowed to cocoon themselves by opting out of taxes or insurance.

In November 2009 at the height of the process that led to the Affordable Care Act, the House Republican leadership issued a fact sheet titled "Republicans' Common-Sense Reforms Will LOWER HEALTH CARE COSTS" [all caps in original]. The GOP plan was billed as a step-by-step approach to reform, contrasted with "Nancy Pelosi's costly, 1,990-page government takeover of our nation's health care system." The first item on their 11-point agenda was to lower health insurance premiums. No elaboration on how this would be achieved, it was just left as a bald assertion. The implied contrast was that Nancy Pelosi and her evil band of Democrats took nearly 2,000 pages to drive up Americans' health costs, whereas the Republicans could save us money on our premiums with just a two-sentence bullet point.

Given that the House Republicans were railing against governmental overreach, it is a little jarring to see such a definitive edict about the price of our private health insurance. And it only becomes more puzzling when you read the rest of the bullet points. The 2009 Republican plan would have offered coverage to those with preexisting medical conditions and banned insurers from setting annual and lifetime spending caps. Sound familiar?

Obviously the Republicans' game was to co-opt the popular parts of Obamacare. But that leaves a couple of major problems for their argument. For one thing, it is hard to characterize coverage of preexisting conditions or the lifting of spending caps as cost-saving measures. Sure, they certainly save money for the consumer—by shifting the risk (and cost) to the insurer. To the extent that preexisting conditions are handled by corralling those with medical needs into high-risk pools, that would shield healthy people from higher costs but would put more on the shoulders of either the unhealthy or the government, depending on the subsidy. The most laughable section of the 2009 fact sheet, though, was the summary scorecard at the bottom:

Scorecard: Speaker Pelosi's Government Takeover vs. GOP Common-Sense Solutions	Speaker Pelosi's Bill	GOP Alternative
Job Losses	Up to 5.5 million	0
Medicare Cuts	$500 billion	0
Tax Increases	$729.5 billion	0

These bottom-line assessments are crude, to put it mildly, and the zeroes in the GOP column are more self-congratulatory rhetoric than fiscal analysis. It is probably safe to assume the fact sheet wasn't run through the Congressional Budget

Office, whose scoring process produces authoritative estimates of the expected budgetary impact of draft legislation. So what the heck, why not claim zero tax increases, job losses, or Medicare cuts as a result of your proposals?

Meanwhile it is worth pausing to focus on those $500 billion in purported Medicare cuts because of an irony of this implicit slam against Pelosicare / Obamacare. The implication is that Obamacare would siphon healthcare dollars from Medicare and consequently shortchange the seniors who rely on it. (In the 2012 election this was one of the Republicans' main line of attacks, citing a higher figure of $700 billion.) Going back to the House GOP plan's main selling point, it promised to "LOWER HEALTH COSTS." Which makes it strange for them to criticize these hundreds of billions of dollars of what are actually cost-saving steps the ACA put in place.

As the political fact-checkers pointed out repeatedly, the Republicans were distorting reform measures that took money from away from healthcare providers rather than Medicare beneficiaries. To get the full ironic effect, though, think of all the times we have heard Republicans talk solemnly about the financial threats to Medicare's future survival. These cheap shots at $500-700 billion in Medicare "cuts" expose the GOP position as being driven by pure political expedience.

Besides all this dodging and darting, the Republican attempt to cherry pick the good parts of Obamacare is also at odds with the libertarian philosophy on which their approach is supposedly based. If requiring coverage for preexisting conditions and prohibiting lifetime caps don't constitute government interference in the market, then what does? As discussed earlier, insurance companies relied those limits on coverage to ensure their profitability, which you'd expect to be sacrosanct under the laissez-faire approach. So when Republicans support these elements of Obamacare, it is a tacit admission that getting government out of the way won't

really force insurance companies to compete for consumers'
business with amazing deals.

The Uninsured Will Always Be With Us

The expansion of Medicaid is second only to the individual mandate as an object of right wing Obamacare hatred.
Shortly after the House Republicans issued their healthcare
reform plan-in-a-fact-sheet, the governors from their party
all put out press releases decrying House passage of the ACA.
While the governors' statements warned of the many hor-
rors Obamacare would bring, many of them homed in on the
impact of new Medicaid beneficiaries on their state budgets.
The following passage from then-Louisiana Governor Bobby
Jindal is a good example:

> Estimates show that the bill will cost our state around $345
> million per year, starting the first year of the full 10 percent
> state match. This added cost has to be absorbed by the state,
> while also adding 360,000 new Medicaid enrollees to the
> Medicaid program, as the new federal mandate requires.
> These additional enrollees do not include the unknown
> number of people that are eligible today for Medicaid but
> not enrolled in the program. Under this new mandate, all
> of those individuals would now also be required to enroll.

Such compassion for the less fortunate! How can one
read it and not be moved? But seriously, Jindal focused so
narrowly on the fiscal impact of the ACA that he completely ignored the human toll. If you were unfamiliar with the
context, you wouldn't know that Jindal was talking about
his state's lowest-income citizens—specifically those without health coverage. Then at the end of the passage comes a
heartwarming sentiment one could paraphrase as, 'how can
Louisiana be expected to expand Medicaid when there are

still eligible poor people who have not yet signed up.'

As the GOP gubernatorial outrage chorus indicates, Medicaid is a joint federal-state program with terms that Obamacare altered. The states have always set their own eligibility requirements, with pre-ACA Medicaid focused on children, pregnant women, mothers of small children, persons with disabilities, and low-income elderly. The costs of care are covered jointly by the state and federal governments. The federal portion averages just over half, but ranges higher or lower depending on the economic strength or weakness of the given state. The Affordable Care Act established a new national income threshold of 138 percent of the poverty line for anyone under the age of 65. Since the authority to enact new qualifications for Medicaid rested with the states, the Obamacare law prodded them to expand coverage by withholding all federal Medicaid support from any states failing to make the change. Yet the ACA offered a positive incentive as well. For the new set of beneficiaries the federal government would pay 90 percent of the costs—after, that is, a gradual phase-in period of several years during which Washington's share go down from 100 to 93 percent (hence Gov. Jindal's reference to the first year in which states would be responsible for 10 percent).

Here we see the partisan asymmetry of healthcare policy: Democrats are trying to help people without health insurance get covered, while Republicans are withholding coverage for the uninsured. The Medicaid expansion was litigated all the way to the Supreme Court, where it lost. In a nutshell, the Republican governors successfully defended states' rights to keep their uninsured citizens off the Medicaid rolls.

The Court's 2012 ruling in *National Federation of Independent Businesses v. Sebelius* largely upheld the constitutionality of Obamacare but struck down, on grounds of federalism, the pivotal provision of Medicaid expansion. At issue was the prod that the ACA used to get states to broaden their qualifying criteria for Medicaid—i.e. the withdrawal of federal government funding. In terms of legal principles governing the federal-state relationship, there is a crucial difference between Washington offering incentives to induce state governments to take a certain step versus coercing states to do so. A majority of seven justices decided that holding back all of the federal government's contribution toward Medicaid fell into the latter category of coercion, and was thus unconstitutional.

But the finer points of intergovernmental relations in our federal system of governance takes us off our real topic of how Republicans deal with the uninsured. Bobby Jindal made it very clear that he viewed 360,000 more Louisianans with health coverage as a problem, if not an outright disaster (and he was hardly the only Republican governor to take this view). Fortunately for Louisianans, Jindal's Democratic successor Gov. John Bel Edward reversed course and expanded Medicaid in their state on his second day in office. Meanwhile here in Wisconsin, the combination of Gov. Scott Walker's partial expansion and refusal of federal funds is costing state taxpayers an extra $323 million during the current budget biennium, while still withholding Medicaid coverage from 83,000 Wisconsinites.

Other Republican governors have supported the expansion—including some who had previously been staunch opponents—but this hardly represents an outbreak of moderation in the party that has defined itself by opposition to Obamacare. For one thing, a number of those GOP governors are in states that lean heavily Democratic. In fact the 2016 presidential candidates within that group, Ohio's John Kasich and Chris Christie of New Jersey, were viewed suspiciously by activists in the Republican base who considered them RINOs. For a fuller picture of how the Tea Party base has asserted itself on this issue, the struggles of other governors trying to expand Medicaid are instructive. Republican governors in South Dakota, Tennessee, Utah, and Wyoming have made proposals for expansion, only to be thwarted by legislators from their own party (who in turn were egged on by groups tied to the Koch brothers).

Meanwhile, we should also note an alibi Republicans often use to prove they aren't as heartless toward the uninsured as they seem. Mitt Romney explained it in an interview on 60 Minutes at the height of the last election season:

> Well we do provide care for people who don't have insurance. If someone has a heart attack, they don't sit in their apartment and die. We pick them up in an ambulance and take them to the hospital and give them care. And different states have different ways of providing for that care. Some provide that care through clinics. Some provide the care through emergency rooms. In my state, we found a solution that worked for my state. But I wouldn't take what we did in Massachusetts and say to Texas, "You've got to take the Massachusetts model."

A strange concept of access to healthcare, to say the least. Just like every other Republican who has trotted out this argument—from George W. Bush to Mitch McConnell and Jim DeMint—Romney omitted a crucial piece. To tell the whole story about access to care for the uninsured, Romney should have added, 'We don't diagnose or treat the heart condition until it becomes a life-or-death emergency.' Later in this chapter we will meet a young fellow Wisconsinite (and repentant Republican) whose case shows the real-life ramifications of this approach.

The reference to Massachusetts, Texas, and the need for states to have autonomy in healthcare brings us to the familiar Republican chestnut about selling insurance across state lines—echoed by Donald Trump, with his customary flair, as "we've got to get rid of the lines around the states." This part of the right wing argument on healthcare reform is an entire variety pack of incoherence. As a general matter regulation of insurance is a prerogative of states. There is no federal law prohibiting an insurance company in one state from selling its wares in another state; it simply has to comply with state insurance regulations in any state where it does business. And when you think about it, the points about state autonomy and selling across state lines are in direct contradiction. If each state needs the ability to tailor healthcare to its unique local circumstances, that would actually argue for keeping "the lines." To reiterate, though, this is a matter of the governmental level that traditionally regulates insurance, rather than the right wing's bogus notion of a top-down fiat.

There are also other questions about how such cross-border insurance markets would work, and whether they would yield the benefits Republicans promise for consumers. Once again it has to do with the insurance companies' standard playbook of cutting the price by skimping on coverage and/or confining themselves to a favorable risk pool of healthy customers. If you give companies their choice of the jurisdiction in which they will operate, will they pick the state with the strongest consumer-oriented regulations or the rules that are most favorable for the insurer? There is no mystery here; getting rid of the lines would trigger a race to the bottom, not the top. Actually we have already seen this movie in the consumer credit industry. The selling of credit cards across state lines is the reason so many of our Visa and MasterCards are issued in Delaware and South Dakota, states that lured consumer finance companies with the country's most lax regulations. And then one final point about the practicalities of selling health insurance across state lines. The biggest practical barrier for an insurer to enter a new region isn't state regulation but rather the task of setting up a local network of healthcare providers—hospitals and doctors who would accept the insurance plan.

Barack Obama, Transformational Figure for Republican Positions on Healthcare

We have seen how hard it is to square laissez-faire rhet-oric about unleashing competitive forces on behalf consum-ers with the real world where customers are at the mercy of insurance companies. It's why Republicans talk a good game about deregulated markets with insurers competing for your business and then hypocritically cherry pick the popular parts of Obamacare, which happen to be regulatory inter-ventions in the marketplace. The asymmetric polarization of the healthcare reform debate is a function of the profound incoherence of the Republican position—only getting worse as the Party's leaders have swerved all over the place. Along the way, they have renounced nearly every sensible approach to the issue. Part of the problem has been Obama derange-ment; the impulse to put President Obama at a maximum political distance has led them to abandon proposals origi-nated by conservatives themselves.

Most famously, the individual insurance mandate was hatched by the Heritage Foundation in the late-1980s, served as a key element of Senate Republican proposals in the 1990s, and then was central to the Massachusetts reform plan en-acted under then-Governor Mitt Romney in the mid-2000s. Long before the mandate became an affront to liberty, con-servatives actually promoted it under the heading of personal responsibility. In fact, Governor Romney called the individ-ual mandate, "the ultimate conservative idea, which is that people have responsibility for their own care, and they don't look to government." Back in the pre-Obama era Romney also sang a different tune when it came to uninsured patients in hospital emergency rooms, describing them as a free-rider problem rather than as last-resort healthcare.

This abandonment of Heritage's proposal inspired the

writer and political analyst Jonathan Chait to attach the famous think tank's name to his theory of a recurring cycle that
predetermines...

> the fate of every Republican health-care plan, a durable
> pattern I call the Heritage Uncertainty Principle. Repub-
> lican health-care proposals reside in a state of quasi-exis-
> tence, and any attempt to summon them into political real-
> ity will cause them to disappear. Their purpose is to refute
> the accusation that Republicans lack a health-care plan.
> The elusive quasi-plan allows them to claim all the poten-
> tial benefits of health-care reform without having to defend
> any drawbacks.[2]

Chait was borrowing one of the laws of physics, the Heisen-
berg Uncertainty Principle, which says the precise location
of subatomic particles cannot be specified at any given time.
In other words, the particles will elude any investigation
into their exact whereabouts, forcing scientists to depict the
structure of atoms in terms of the distributed probability
of the particles' locations. Of course this isn't an option for
healthcare policy makers, whose reform plans must be clear
and specific in order to be feasible.

The difficulty of translating right wing orthodoxy into
implementable reforms is underscored when you compare
the 2009 House GOP factsheet with later proposals from
conservatives in Congress, statehouses, and think tanks. John
McDonough and Max Fletcher at Harvard's TH Chan School
of Public Health very helpfully compiled a chart summariz-
ing eight proposed Obamacare replacements issued between
late-2012 and mid-2015.[3] The period of February-March
2015 was particularly active, with the unveiling of the Health
Care Choice Act from Senators Barrasso, Crapo, Cruz, Rubio, and Vitter as well as the Patient CARE Act by Senators
Burr and Hatch along with Representative Fred Upton. As
significant substantive differences with the 2009 fact sheet,

just one of the conservative proposals guarantees coverage for preexisting conditions (none of the congressional proposals did) and only two proposals eliminated lifetime spending caps (one of those being the Burr-Hatch-Upton bill). The latest proposal to come out, from House Speaker Paul Ryan as part of his "A Better Way" working paper series, once again left out guaranteed coverage for preexisting conditions (camouflaging that gap with protection for those with continuous coverage). This shift at least has the virtue of being consistent with the Republicans' belief in deregulation. But good luck trying to sell the American public on a return to the worst aspects of pre-Obamacare health insurance. Which brings us back to Jon Chait's Heritage Uncertainty Principle and the near certainty these proposals will never really be pushed by their authors.

Due to a combination of ideology and antipathy toward President Obama, Republicans have veered away from certain conservative principles in healthcare reform that they could instead be affirming. In other words, there is plenty for conservatives to love in the ACA, beyond the personal responsibility of the individual mandate. For instance, if Republicans weren't so quick to condemn health insurance exchanges as a government takeover of healthcare, they might see that the exchanges promote exactly the kind of consumer empowerment and freedom of choice conservatives say they want. The purpose of the exchanges—which are meant for individuals, families, and small businesses—is to show consumers their options for different levels of coverage. The insurance plans on the exchanges are all offered by private companies, which are essentially competing for customers' business. The governmental role is to provide a framework to standardize key elements of the coverage and clarify the information consumers use as a basis for their choices.

Again, this is only an intrusion if you think consumers and insurers are truly on an equal footing in an unregulated marketplace. Conservatives are always warning against the arrogant presumption that government knows what is best for us. But the flip side of their suspicion of government is a trust in the private sector that seems pretty naïve. To say that we consumers are in the best position to know our own needs and preferences doesn't tell the whole story of healthcare. Insurance companies also know what is best for their bottom-line interests. And just like credit card companies, mortgage bankers, and investment advisors, they can trick consumers by burying things in the fine print of their insurance policies.

From the progressive vantage, then, the point is not that government knows what's best for us; it's that the government knows about the ways insurers can make things worse for us. So rather than depriving consumers of choice, Obamacare's insurance exchanges set up markets that consumers can easily navigate to find the plans that suit them. Their four standard levels of coverage (bronze, silver, gold, platinum) help consumers make apples-to-apples comparisons among all the different products.

Then there was the outcry over the supposed "death panels" provision in the draft version of the ACA, a controversy instigated by the GOP's former vice presidential candidate and ace provocateur: Sarah Palin. A few weeks after stepping down as Alaska governor, Palin stoked the right wing's Summer 2009 frenzy of Obamacare fear-mongering by seizing on a section of the House bill (Section 1233) that provided Medicare reimbursements when doctors counsel their patients on end-of-life care—basically the advance directives (or living wills) that make the patients' own wishes known. The bill didn't require physicians to give counseling on living wills; it merely classified such consultations as reimbursable services under Medicare.

One might be forgiven for being perplexed about the supposed government takeover entailed here. Outside of the camp that views Obamacare as an expressway to tyranny, these kinds of intimate conversations would seem to be the essence of the sacred doctor-patient relationship. Indeed prior to the summer of 2009, extending coverage for end-of-life counseling was so uncontroversial it was one of the very few healthcare reform measures to have genuine bipartisan support. So the argument here seems completely backwards. Surely it is the Republicans who have let government intrude on our freedom of choice as healthcare consumers.

With this low point in the healthcare reform debate in mind, let's return for a moment to the larger problem that is the subject of this book: America's political discourse is coming unmoored from reality. What does it say about the state of our governance when one of the US Senate's most experienced members, Chuck Grassley of Iowa, described Section 1233 as a "government-run plan to decide when to pull the plug on grandma?" Grassley was piling one gross distortion on top of another. Let us not forget that using government-run plan to describe reforms largely based on private insurance is just as mendacious. It's as if the Republicans, having gotten away with the older distortion for so long, proceeded to blow right through to the next big lie—one that demonizes the president and his party as granny-killers.

On so many issues these days, Republicans take a hedonistic political approach; if it feels politically advantageous, do it. God bless the fact-checking services such as Politifact, but their efforts are badly mismatched to the scale of the problem. For instance, consider how pundits and the media say that the politics are bad for some issue. Often this is just another way of saying the facts and merits of the matter have been overtaken by manipulation and distortion. The unpopularity of Obamacare is a case in point. Heck, if the Affordable Care Act did all the things that its critics allege, I would be against it too. Also bear in mind that a segment of the popular distaste for the law comes not from the right wing, but from the left—Americans who think Obamacare didn't go far enough.

Were Republicans Always This Clueless?

The idea of asymmetric polarization implies a claim that the ideological tunnel vision of today's Republicans is a departure from bygone days of conservative pragmatism. For the topic at hand, has Jonathan Chait's Heritage Uncertainty Principle always required that Republican healthcare reform proposals were nothing more than politically expedient gimmicks? Do Republicans have any record of offering meaningful solutions?

Looking back to the early-1970s, Richard Nixon's healthcare policy stance in his last few years as president serves as a data point for past Republican reasonableness. The concerns of that period as well as the policy remedies under consideration will all seem familiar. As the eminent historian of American health care Paul Starr recounts, spiraling healthcare costs stirred enough worry to rise to the top of the political agenda. Between the late-1950s and the late-1960s, medical inflation spiked from 3.2 to 7.9 percent.[4]

President Nixon put out his first major healthcare proposal in 1971, but he couldn't build enough bipartisan consensus to get any real traction. Three years later, though, Nixon offered a new proposal and sought to hash out a compromise with Senator Ted Kennedy and House Ways and Means Committee Chair Wilbur Mills. The Nixon plan included a mandate for employers to provide insurance for their workers—the same employer mandate that today's conservatives promised would be a devastating job-killer (it hasn't been). The plan also had guaranteed coverage for preexisting conditions, a cap on policyholders' out-of-pocket expenses, and government program to replace Medicaid that would cover Americans at any income level who were unable to obtain private insurance. In the end, the possibility of enacting reform was doomed by Nixon's own political demise in 1974. To be sure, the mounting Watergate scandal gave Nixon added motive to seek a substantive achievement by pushing healthcare reform through Congress. But that doesn't detract from the point being made here: a Republican president pursued reality-based reforms with provisions his conservative successors slammed as tyrannical.

Nor was this the final instance of constructive Republican participation in the healthcare reform debate. The next round came in 1993-94 when a Democrat was in the White House and faced competing reform proposals from congressional Republicans. The biggest rival plan to President Bill Clinton's own healthcare reform package was a Senate bill put forward by Rhode Island's Senator John Chafee along with 18 other Republicans. Unlike the Nixon plan's emphasis on an employer mandate, the Chafee bill centered on an individual insurance mandate. The reforms in the leading Republican-sponsored bill in the House, offered by Representative Jim Cooper of Tennessee, were less sweeping than the Senate bill. Yet the Cooper bill also shared a key element of Obamacare. It proposed to standardize private insurance plans, require them to offer adequate coverage, and market them to consumers on government-run health insurance exchanges. Fast forward to the Obama era, and the Republican response to the exchanges was to refuse to set them up in many states—thus leaving it to Washington to do it for them—and then seize on clumsy wording in the Affordable Care Act to mount a legal challenge to federal authority to establish exchanges in those states.

Ultimately the Clinton reform push marked the death knell of bipartisan cooperation on healthcare. It was also the dawn of right wing obstructionism and ideological purism, with William Kristol supplying the Ur text in the form of a December 1993 strategy memo outlining his recommended

Republican response.[5] As Kristol saw it, defeating the Clinton healthcare plan was vital to the Republicans' political fortunes and the future of the conservative cause. While the proposed reforms would eventually lead to the rationing of care and put the government between us and our doctors, in the meantime Kristol feared they would burnish Democrats' image as problem-solvers and make the government look like a source of solutions. This left Republicans with just one option: an "aggressive and uncompromising counterstrategy designed to delegitimize the proposal and defeat its partisan purpose."

One could hardly ask for a better example than Kristol's memo to highlight the asymmetric polarization of healthcare reform. In purely partisan terms, the memo indeed served Republican political interests very well. But when you look to Kristol's paper for a policy response to America's healthcare challenge, what you find is … a short-term political strategy plus a few half-measures and pipedreams. This was an early glimpse of the fallacy of laissez-faire health care. After listing a number of modest near-term reforms such as coverage of preexisting conditions, tax deductibility of insurance premiums for the unemployed, and subsidized clinics in underserved rural and urban areas, Kristol noted that:

> These may only be intermediate measures. A more ambitious agenda of free-market reforms remains open for the future: medical IRAs, tax credits and vouchers for insurance, and the like.

To appreciate the ramifications of Kristol's "more ambitious agenda," it helps to step back and look at it in the context of his overall argument. The main thrust of the memo is that Republicans can better protect the middle class by getting the government off their backs than Democrats can serve middle class interests via governmental action. In fact, Kristol took aim at the Clinton administration's conceptual frame and the attempt to sell their plan on the grounds of providing *security* against the dangers of a dysfunctional healthcare system. The key to the Kristol strategy was to contrast Clinton's abstract notion of the health system with Americans' own direct experiences with healthcare at an individual level. He argued Clintoncare would wreak havoc for people who were basically happy with their medical care.

Now let's look at what the more ambitious Republican agenda would do. These free-market reforms are all in the same spirit as the notion of the empowered consumer. Here again we have the fallacy that ordinary Americans would get a better healthcare bargain by serving as the direct purchasers of medical care—with the money put in our hands instead of the insurance companies or government bureaucrats.

There is a problem, though, if consumers' vaunted purchasing power falls short and leaves them unable to afford the care they need. This is the difficulty with a healthcare program that gives people a defined dollar amount contribution instead of a defined benefit of coverage for medical services. What if the voucher or the balance in a medical savings account isn't enough? That question might sound familiar from the 2012 presidential election when attention focused on a proposal by Rep. Paul Ryan (then the GOP nominee for vice president) to shift Medicare to a defined contribution program, using what Ryan euphemistically called "premium support."

Returning to the Kristol memo, in one breath it lambastes the Clinton reforms as horribly disruptive to people's medical care and in the next breath proposes a radical change in how (actually whether) their coverage will be paid for. Notwithstanding Kristol's objections to the word security, that is exactly what is at stake in this debate, and Republican proposals offer less of it.

Kristol accused then-First Lady Hillary Clinton of

fear-mongering when she "routinely describes a nation of individual lives teetering on the brink, each only an illness or a job switch away from financial ruin." And here we should highlight policy measures that were notable for their absence in the Kristol strategy: coverage for individuals faced with extremely high medical bills. As long as insurers were allowed to limit the total they would pay in a year or over a lifetime— something newly prohibited under Obamacare—individuals were indeed threatened by the financial ruin Hillary Clinton warned of. To reiterate, prior to the Affordable Care Act medical bills were the leading cause of personal bankruptcy in America.

"If you like your healthcare, keep your healthcare."

From 1993 onward, the Republican healthcare agenda has been confined to very limited objectives. Aside from bipartisan efforts on CHIP programs to cover children and the prescription drug coverage President George W. Bush added to Medicare, none of the conservatives' proposals have offered serious reality-based solutions to the problems of the uninsured, underinsured, or rapidly escalating medical costs. Instead their function has been to conjure the specter of government overreach, echo clichés about the free market, and keep from imposing any burden on those who are happy with the status quo. In that third task, the Republicans have been well aligned with the structure of American healthcare politics, which scholar Paul Starr has called a "health policy trap" and defined as follows:

> [A] costly and complicated system that has left a growing minority of Americans without financial protection in sickness but has nonetheless satisfied enough people to make it difficult to change.[6]

For Republicans this doesn't represent a trap so much as a warm and comfortable political place. In William Kristol's memo, the height of irony is when he characterizes his strategy as an "appeal to the enlightened self-interest of middle-class America." Yet there is nothing enlightened about encouraging the healthcare 'haves' in our society to guard against hyped-up threats and leave the 'have-nots' out in the cold.

As with the other three fallacies, the myth of laissez-faire healthcare works to the disadvantage of the more honest of the two political parties. The party that has worked pragmatically to address the gaps in the American healthcare system—wrestling with the complexities and tradeoffs—is stuck in an unfair fight with political opponents who do nothing more than spew deceptive and simplistic nonsense. Because moving to a true government-run single-payer system would indeed be too radical of a shift, Democrats made the sensible choice to base their reform program mainly on private health insurance. But that didn't stop Republicans from keeping shouting 'government takeover!' How do you counter such a smear when the nonpartisan arbiters of the political class fail to call bullshit on it—when Republicans' major-party status gives them a megaphone regardless of the veracity of their arguments?

For President Obama the answer was a message to the healthcare 'haves' that the reforms aren't about them. Since the Affordable Care Act was aimed mainly at the uninsured, those who have coverage would largely be unaffected. In his speeches, the president conveyed this reassurance with variants of the line "if you like your healthcare, you can keep your healthcare." Despite what the critics said, Obamacare would not snatch private insurance plans away from people in a socialistic grab for control. The president's boiled-down encapsulation of healthcare reform was not, however, meant as a blanket promise that every American would be able to keep whatever plan she had. A small percentage of the insured population—particularly individuals and families who purchase their own plans—were bound to have policies cancelled on them.

Politically this became a high-profile issue in the fall of 2013, when hundreds of thousands of people received cancellation notices from their insurers just as the websites for the new government-hosted insurance exchanges were being prepared. The websites were themselves a problem and took several months to be fixed and work properly. That left millions of people in the dark for a period, but the discontinuation of their old policies was less scandalous than it seemed. As the *Washington Post*'s Sarah Kliff noted in an excellent explainer on this issue, "The cancellation notices are a feature of the Affordable Care Act, not a bug. The idea was to make insurance coverage more robust—and that means cancelling policies that offer less thorough coverage."[7]

If you judge healthcare reform solely on whether it leaves people's insurance untouched—as most Republicans seem to do—then the withdrawal of these policies might count as disastrous. Homing in on such a narrow question, though, means ignoring some big pieces of the problem. Before Obamacare insurance companies could refuse to cover people with preexisting conditions, sharply limit the services covered (e.g. pregnancy and childbirth), and limit the dollar amount of claims paid in a year or a lifetime (leaving the policyholder on the hook for tens or hundreds of thousands of dollars). Given that Obamacare fills those gaps in everyone's private insurance policies, it's hard to see what outrage is supposedly being perpetrated on the American people. When you boil it down, the right wing critique is simply that the government is doing something. They won't come right out and say it, but the Republicans are implicitly arguing that insurance companies take our interests to heart better than our government does. As I say, the point of healthcare reform isn't that the government knows what's best for us, just that they know the tricks of the health insurance trade better than we do.

"This chump gets a second shot at life"

One of the best poster boys for the Affordable Care Act is a Central Wisconsin Republican who lives about 20 miles from me. In June 2015, Brent Brown of Mosinee wrote President Obama to say what the ACA has meant to him. Nine months later, Brent was asked to introduce the president at a healthcare-focused event in Milwaukee. In his letter and statements for the event, Brown spoke candidly about his own medical and political history. As his letter says:

> I was very vocal in my opposition to you—particularly the ACA. Before I briefly explain my story allow me to first say this: I am so very sorry. I was so very wrong.

Brown had a serious autoimmune disease, a preexisting condition that made it impossible for him to get health insurance. He received much of his healthcare in the emergency room because he would avoid seeking help until it was a matter of life and death. With nothing left of his savings, Brown had no way to pay for the expensive surgery and medicine needed to manage his condition and stay alive. The ACA made all the difference for Brown. Under Obamacare he gained access to care he described as having previously been "hidden behind a doctor's apology: 'I'm sorry, Mr. Brown, we have to take your financial consideration into account.'" Introducing President Obama in Milwaukee, Brown summarized his reassessment of the president by saying:

> I am a Republican who cursed his name, and falsely accused him, and zealously worked to ensure that he would

never be my president. But thanks to his fortitude, thanks
to his unwavering vision of mercy—even towards me—this
chump gets a second shot at life.

As Brown's case shows, the most powerful weapon
against the slanderously misrepresented GOP version of the
Affordable Care Act is the actual ACA. Indeed, it is a sign of
Republican weakness on these issues that they have resorted to such wild distortions. By the time Congress passed the
ACA, the most practical and palatable approach to healthcare reform was fairly clear—at least in its contours—from
the previous rounds of debate and modified positions of key
players like the insurance industry. Democrats worked within that framework and made the first major stride toward
universal healthcare in 45 years. Republicans refused to take
part in shaping the legislation and then blamed Democrats
for failing to obtain bipartisan support, much like the mur-
derer who pleads for sympathy as an orphan after killing his
parents.

And because Obamacare was basically assembled from
the only elements it could have been, the GOP's rejection-
ist stance left it without a substantive healthcare platform to
stand on. The ACA expanded health coverage and protected
against medical bill-induced bankruptcy in the only way it
could, through a combination of individual and employer
mandates, Medicaid expansion, and new insurance regulations and exchanges. When Republicans stiffened their opposition to any governmental role in healthcare reform, all
that remained was their laissez-faire fantasy of a Carmax for
heart surgery.

Looking to the years ahead, what is the possibility of a
less polarized health policy discourse? The Affordable Care
Act hardly cured all the ills of American healthcare. There
are still a number of serious challenges to be addressed, and
moderate conservative perspectives might have some salient

insights. Still, we should not underestimate the shift that would be required for Republicans to engage constructively. The fallacy of the hard-bargaining consumer with skin in the game won't be any more useful in the next phase of the debate than it was in the last. Republicans must stop perseverating on their pet proposals: health savings-accounts, Medicare vouchers (sorry, "premium support"), high-risk pools, and high-deductible or catastrophic health insurance. Above all, they must abandon their obsessive and counterproductive crusade to repeal Obamacare. Is this a lot to ask of Republicans? Sure it is. But there is no way around it, the onus falls on the ideologues to come back down to earth.

Bending the Cost Curve

With all that said, it should be music to Republican ears that the next major health policy challenge is an efficiency problem. Given the enormous sums our country spends in this outsized economic sector, we don't get very good value for the money. In fact, it is a misnomer to talk about our healthcare system when what we really have is a medical treatment system. The roots of the problem run so deep that way back in 1971 President Nixon described it in his national health strategy in terms that are still apt today:

In most cases our present medical system operates episodically—people come to it in moments of distress—when they require its most expensive services. Yet both the system and those it serves would be better off if less expensive services could be delivered on a more regular basis.

If more of our resources were invested in preventing sickness and accidents, fewer would have to be spent on costly cures. If we gave more attention to treating illness in its early stages, then we would be less troubled by acute disease. In short, we should build a true "health" system—and not a "sickness" system alone. We should work to maintain health and not merely to restore it.

This brings us to the portion of the debate where conservatives are partly correct. Our current system is skewed toward cost growth rather than restraint in spending. There is indeed a problem of the overuse of medical services because the cost is pushed onto a third party such as an insurance company or the government. The conservatives' mistake, however, lies in blaming the consumer as the source of the problem when the provider is actually at fault.

As we said in discussing the doctor-patient relationship at the beginning of this chapter, it is unrealistic to expect the patient to drive a hard bargain over the cost of her treatment. The same *New Yorker* article in which Atul Gawande drew the contrast between healthcare and buying a rug in a souk, "The Cost Conundrum," delved into the vexed challenge of medical inflation.[8] As a window into the problem Gawande compared two similar South Texas cities, McAllen and El Paso, with very different price tags for local medical care. Based on Gawande's reporting, the key driver of McAllen's high costs—the second highest per patient in the entire country—was the local doctors' penchant for recommending expensive tests and surgeries. This dysfunction in American medicine has also been recognized for many decades and was highlighted in the same 1971 Nixon health strategy:

> Under traditional systems, doctors and hospitals are paid, in effect, on a piece work basis. The more illnesses they treat—and the more service they render—the more their income rises. This does not mean, of course, that they do any less than their very best to make people well. But it does mean that there is no economic incentive for them to concentrate on keeping people healthy.

As an example of perverse incentives, consider repeated stays in a hospital. When a patient returns to the hospital after a recent stay, that would often indicate a failure on the part of that hospital. On a purely fee-for-service basis, though, such readmissions add to the institution's bottom line. The Affordable Care Act dealt with this problem by instituting new penalties for excessive readmissions. For more than 3,000 hospitals that treat significant numbers of Medicare-covered patients, the federal government's Centers for Medicare and Medicaid Services (CMS) set the bar for the number of patients those hospitals could reasonably be expected to readmit within 30 days of being discharged. Hospitals exceeding their designated benchmark are penalized with a reduction in their total Medicare reimbursement that ranges from a fraction of a percent to a maximum three percent. (The ACA uses Medicare's payment system and the CMS as test beds for numerous experiments in healthcare reform.)

The penalties have been levied against more than 2,500 hospitals, the great majority of institutions that come under the program, but they have also had the desired effect on readmissions. In the first few years of the program, the overall rate of readmission declined from more than 19 percent to under 18 percent—representing approximately 150,000 Medicare patients nationwide. The program has not been free of controversy, however. Some hospitals have protested that the program's benchmarks fail to account for the socioeconomic status of the patients they serve. It's true that patients with lower levels of income and/or education may be less diligent about the instructions they received when the hospital discharged them, though CMS rebuts this by pointing to the success of similar institutions with fewer readmissions. Another debate has questioned whether hospitals are gaming the system by keeping patients under observation rather than admitting them.

The ACA instituted a similar penalty system for so-called hospital-acquired conditions—instances when hospitals actually worsened the health of patients under their care. One major subset here is hospitals' too-frequent failure to protect patients from picking up new infections. The penalties for these failures also shave off a small percentage of Medicare reimbursements, but in this program the sanction is applied to all hospitals graded in the bottom 25 percent of the class. With some of the most respected institutions in the country failing this test (including the Cleveland Clinic), it isn't clear whether CMS is using the right methodology. Is there a better alternative for CMS to track performance than the billing code data they currently use? Still, the new incentives have had unprecedented success in combating the problem. Hospital-acquired conditions fell by 17 percent nationally between 2010-2013, saving an estimated 50,000 lives and $12 billion.

Other ACA provisions tackle American medicine's dominant fee-for-service model head-on, by reforming the way that medical care is paid for or that physicians organize their practice. Treating patients on a fee-for-service basis atomizes healthcare—splitting and spreading it among disparate primary care providers, specialists, technicians, hospitals, and outpatient centers. It is not a system geared to steer a patient along a straight path to good health. Our current system isn't set up to draw a team of professionals together in the patient's corner and base her treatment on medicine's latest wisdom. A number of ACA reforms try to nudge things in that direction.

Bundled payments, for instance, give healthcare providers a set amount of money for a certain medical treatment such as a knee or hip replacements. Since it is a system based on providers' assumed ability to cut costs, CMS takes 3 percent off the top (gauged against the typical cost). Then if the providers succeed in lowering the cost even further, they get to pocket the additional savings. Conversely, they are on the hook for the overrun if they fail to cut costs. In April 2015 Kaiser Health News told the story of a local hospital chain in San Antonio, Baptist Health System, that used the bundled payments to streamline the knee replacements they performed. When it comes to recognizing the sticker shock of healthcare prices, the article shows that doctors have been late to the party:

> Baptist surgeons, who select which artificial joint to use, were shocked to find out how much more some devices cost than others. Once they had a stake in the total bill, they became more discriminating shoppers. Metal hip and knee prices started plummeting "the second the flashlight got lit on the implant makers," Viroslav said. No manufacturer wanted to be the most expensive.
>
> Surgeons were also surprised to learn that almost half the expense of joint replacement can come from physical therapy, home nurse visits and temporary nursing home stays after the surgery. Dr. David Fox never paid much notice to the birthday cards that rehab nursing homes sent him. Now that the knee-and-hip surgeon knows what they were making on his referrals, "it's no damn wonder" they were so nice, he said. These days, Baptist doctors are likely to order home therapy rather than a nursing home stay unless it's clearly needed. For the nursing homes they do use, they're more likely to stay in touch, coordinate care and reduce expensive readmissions, they say.[9]

Bundled payments depend on close cooperation among the different care providers, and the resulting financial benefit is likewise split between the surgeons and their hospital. Baptist Health would not disclose the percentage they saved on the knee replacements, but they did tell Kaiser Health News that the combined savings of this and another healthcare delivery reform they tried was over $1 million. And it remains to be seen how many different procedures and courses of treatment could be improved through bundled payments.

Looking beyond specific maladies toward patients' over-all health, the Affordable Care Act includes alternative payment systems that encourage doctors to improve the quality of care while lowering cost. The mechanism is the accountable care organization (ACO), a group medical practice that solidifies its commitment to well coordinated, holistic care by putting itself under the same kinds of benchmarks and incentives discussed above. The difference is that the incentives for ACOs have a broader scope and encompass the groups' total care for their Medicare patients.

If an ACO scores well on its quality metrics and shaves more than 2 percent off of the normally anticipated cost benchmark, then group can pocket the excess savings. For a more limited set of "pioneer" ACOs, the payment system is structured to transition away from fee-for-service. If a pioneer ACO cuts costs by at least 2 percent for two years, while maintaining quality, then starting in the third year it can collect a flat amount for each of their Medicare payments. The savings achieved by ACOs in their initial years have been modest—just over a half billion dollars, when you count just the one-quarter of ACOs and half of pioneer ACOs that hit their targets and exclude those that were not as successful in cost-cutting. Perhaps unsurprisingly, the pioneer ACOs have been the most successful part of the program. They were also, by definition, the groups that came to the process well prepared and with a running start. Whatever the disappointment with the attempt at cost-cutting, the ACOs generally performed well on the quality metrics.

Now if all of these payment and delivery reforms seem like experiments, that's because they are. Because no one is sure precisely how to stabilize medical costs, the best course is to try a variety of approaches. President Obama himself acknowledged in his July 2016 article in the *Journal of the American Medical Association* that, "both insurers and policy makers are still learning about the dynamics of an insurance market that includes all people regardless of any pre-existing conditions" particularly when it comes to insurance exchanges where companies have raised rates after setting them too low initially or local areas with very few options to choose.[10]

The seriousness of the problem, though, is beyond question. If we allow healthcare spending to grow faster than the economy, we will end up with a serious imbalance. An outsized healthcare sector is a sign of an unhealthy economy, so to speak. And for all the Republican scaremongering about government debt and deficit and an insolvent Social Security, a high medical inflation rate poses a real threat. Unless brought under control, healthcare costs could threaten the solvency of Medicare and consume a growing share of state and federal budgets. Rather than a government takeover of healthcare, we could see a healthcare takeover of government.

There is good news on this front, though. Since the enactment of Obamacare, medical inflation has gone down dramatically. Looking at the trends in the reimbursement of insurance claims per capita, private insurers have seen the annual rate of increase drop from a range of 4-5 percent in 2000-2010 to just one percent in 2010-2014. On the Medicare side, there has been an absolute decline in spending per patient rather than merely a slowing of inflation—a shift from a 2-4 percent range in the annual medical inflation rate to -0.6 percent more recently.

Can Republicans Come Back Down to Earth?

Again, the point about these unresolved issues of healthcare cost and quality is their suitability as topics for a classic between-the-40-yardlines debate between Democrats and a Republican Party that recovered its senses. As a bonus, Democrats could perhaps throw medical malpractice reform into the bargain. I hasten to add that any reform should preserve meaningful restitution for malpractice victims rather than simply gutting the tort system. But as Ezekiel Emanuel has argued, the realities of the current system do a poor job of making victims whole:

> Even if the cost of defensive medicine to the total health care system is small, the malpractice system is clearly defective. It fails to achieve any of its 3 goals: it does not fairly compensate patients harmed by physician and/or hospital negligence, it does not settle cases quickly or cost effectively, and it holds a guillotine over physicians who are likely to be sued no matter how conscientiously they practice and in which many suits are frivolous.[11]

It is possible to imagine Republicans being interested in a constructive policy debate about how to wring more inefficiencies out of American healthcare. As I say, though, it would require them to shift into a very different mode than they have been. The burden of proof for good faith is squarely on them. If Republicans only want to rail against Obamacare, scream 'government takeover!' and throw consumers into the marketplace without protections or resources, then there will be no meaningful healthcare reform debate.

Judging by their actions in the past decade, the political leaders who set Republican policy do not really see any serious problems with contemporary American healthcare. Strip away the talking points about health savings accounts and high-risk pools—which by now seem like such a rote recital I wonder whether the politicians can even remember their underlying rationale—and the essence of Republican health policy is the preservation of the status quo. More specifically, the GOP's main goal is to make sure nothing is taken away from those Americans who are fortunate to have health coverage.

As with each of the four fallacies, the current asymmetric polarization is a consequence of Republicans having wandered off the reservation of pragmatic policy making. In the process that led to Obamacare, all the political, social, professional, and corporate stakeholders bargained over their interests and ideas. The swap of new private insurance customers via the individual mandate in exchange for coverage of preexisting conditions was one such bargain at the center of the deal. All the stakeholder groups except for one: the Republicans. For a while, a handful of congressional Republicans made a good show of participating in the legislative process, but ultimately not a single one voted for the Affordable Care Act. And as we saw, this put them in the position of disowning their earlier proposals. Under such circumstances, the only honest way to look at bipartisanship is the summary of the ACA drafting process given by then-White House Chief of Staff Rahm Emanuel to the *Washington Post*'s Dana Milbank in June 2009:

> This will be bipartisan; there will be ideas from both parties and individuals from both parties in the final product. Whether Republicans decide to vote for things they promoted will be up to them.[12]

Further Reading

Brill, Steven. *America's Bitter Pill: Money, Politics, Backroom Deals, and the Fight to Fix Our Broken Healthcare System*. New York: Random House, 2015.

Emanuel, Ezekiel J. *Reinventing American Healthcare: How the Affordable Care Act Will Improve our Terribly Complex, Blatantly Unjust, Outrageously Expensive, Grossly Inefficient, Error Prone System*. New York: Public Affairs Books, 2014.

Jost, Timothy Stoltzfus. *Health Care At Risk: A Critique of the Consumer-Driven Movement.* Durham: Duke University Press, 2007.

Starr, Paul. *Remedy and Reaction: The Peculiar American Struggle Over Health Care Reform.* New Haven: Yale University Press, 2013.

4

Almighty America

The political divide over foreign policy is essentially a clash of ideas about American global leadership and influence. When you boil down all the debates and issues, Democrats view the United States as powerful while Republicans see our country as all-powerful.

In light of recent history, it's strange to see the GOP offer an international agenda brimming with confidence in their ability to shape the world. When presidential candidate Jeb Bush flubbed multiple attempts to stake a clear position on his brother's 2003 invasion of Iraq, it was a symptom of his party's wider failure to come to terms with that debacle. Very few Republicans would, at this point, defend the Iraq War or deny its tragic costs. Yet even fewer have adjusted their foreign policy approaches and assumptions. Even if they no longer advocate invading large Middle Eastern countries, most of the Republicans' proposals are still premised on op- timistic we'll-be-greeted-as-liberators scenarios that expect everything to go according to plan. More to the point, they anticipate everybody going along with America's plan.

If anything, the Republicans' approach to foreign policy has moved even farther to the right since they became the opposition party. Toward the end of George W. Bush's presidency, the GOP foreign policy establishment was chastened by the ill will and isolation caused by the Iraq War, and they showed signs of moderating. I saw this first-hand in 2007 when I co-led a project that paired up leading Republican and Democratic policy wonks to find common ground in their areas of specialty. In the resulting book, *Bridging the Foreign Policy Divide*, we liberals gave nods toward conservative ideas in which we saw merit, but there was more movement in the other direction. There was bipartisan agreement on the importance of international support and legitimacy for the use of force, the inexcusability of torturing prisoners, and the need for nuclear-armed powers to cut their arsenals, to name a few.[1] Plus, the 2008 presidential campaign included notable moderate positions, such as John McCain signaling his openness to ratifying the Comprehensive Test Ban Treaty that prohibits test detonations of nuclear warheads. And both of the parties' 2008 nominees opposed the use of torture and supported closing Guantanamo.

Unfortunately that was a high water mark for bipartisanship. In the meantime the GOP went back to a foreign policy platform that's been as bullheaded as ever. In the world according to Republicans, the United States should be in full command of events. If other nations or groups act against America's wishes, it is because we haven't done enough to keep them in line. Simply by showing enough fortitude—or resolve, a key magic word of right wing rhetoric—the U.S. can domineer everyone else and supposedly get them to behave.

Recall the notion of the four fallacies as a category of basic premises that drive a wedge between right wing ideas and observable reality. On foreign policy and national security, the fantasy that America can bring the rest of the world to heel makes Republicans prone to disastrous ideas. If you believe all of America's aims can be achieved by shows of strength and will, then showing restraint is never appropriate. And because GOP national security arguments never call for a balance of factors, they can lead to unbalanced policy recommendations.

It can even lead to a Republican presidential nominee who has seemed determined—despite the spectacular foreign policy failures of the last administration—to out-Cheney the former vice president himself. In an election season brimming with truly weird debates, surely one of the most bizarre was the scenario of the U.S. military put in the position of having to refuse an unlawful order from a President Trump. In the politics of national security, Donald Trump's pledge to "bring back a hell of a lot worse than waterboarding" and target civilian family members of terrorist figures played off of the image of toughness Republicans have cultivated for years. It isn't that all Republicans want to target civilians or bring back torture (though Trump was one of at least six candidates opposed to keeping prisoner interrogations within tight standards). But the GOP's entire appeal to voters, and critique of Obama foreign policy, has made bold claims for toughness as a cure-all and scoffed at other considerations like international support and legitimacy. The voices of the Republican foreign policy pragmatists have been drowned out by much more strident spokespersons. They no longer have a hand in crafting their party's platform, none of them has supported Donald Trump in 2016, and in fact many said they would vote for Hillary Clinton.

For a number of reasons, though, uniformed servicemembers take the international norms for the treatment of prisoners and the selection of targets very seriously. As a matter of ethics, the rules governing the conduct of armed forces put crucial limits on the warrior's profession and draw a clear line separating it from savagery. The international legal form of those rules are the Geneva Conventions, with international norms also echoed in the U.S. military code, legal system, and other standards of conduct. Because of the rules about minimizing civilian casualties, for instance, military lawyers from the JAG Corps are deployed to make sure civilians are not targeted. For the treatment of prisoners, not only does the U.S. Army Field Manual spell out standards that forbid torture, human rights advocates pushed for those same standards to be used also when civilian intelligence and law enforcement officers interrogate terror suspects. These are the standards that were resisted by six of the 2016 GOP candidates including Jeb Bush, Marco Rubio, and Lindsey Graham (a JAG officer in the Air Force Reserves who ought to know better). And the U.S. military has another good reason for upholding international norms and treating prisoners humanely: they want the same humane treatment when Americans are captured on the battlefield.

Whatever Donald Trump may believe about the powers of the commander in chief, the United States is a nation of laws that constrain even what a president can do. When Trump's waterboarding comments sparked controversy, and he was asked about the military rebuffing orders to commit torture, Trump replied, "They won't refuse. They're not gonna refuse me. Believe me." Even as he offers himself as a potential president, Trump knows less about the issue than a recruit at boot camp. As it says clearly in the Uniform Code of Military Justice, all uniformed personnel are required to refuse any unlawful order from a superior officer.

Again, while Trump has taken the posture of toughness to farther extremes than most other Republican political figures, he took his cues from the party's standard foreign policy messages. It is no great credit to other Republicans that they stop short of shredding the Geneva Conventions. After all, they share the same distaste for international agreements and, like Trump, advocate a foreign policy in which the United States makes all demands and no concessions.

Nor should we read too much into Trump's supposed rejection of GOP foreign policy dogma on trade liberalization, military adventurism, or his impulse to turn America's attention inward. For one thing, his claimed opposition to military interventions is belied by the record of his own statements (as we've learned, Trump has a special knack for revising his views). The commonalities among Republicans are much more important than the differences. As with the other three fallacies covered in this book, the Republicans' core arguments and assumptions pose an obstacle to sound foreign policymaking. The right wing delusion of an Almighty America leads Republicans to offer totally unrealistic proposals and discount any tradeoffs or resistance from other players. In his unique style, Trump has simply taken the standard Republican oversimplifications and made them more cartoonish.

Bar Stool Bluster

For every international challenge of the last eight years, Republicans have claimed they could attain the desired outcome via military aid/maneuvers/threats, economic sanctions, diplomatic isolation, solidarity with allies, and/or refusal to compromise. When right wing politicians or pundits make these proposals, they sound like the tiresome know-it-all you might meet at a party or a bar—inflicting his stock blowhard rant on anyone within earshot. And this is one reason for the low quality of our foreign policy debates: we have grown so used to hearing these ideas that we've become complacent and allow bar stool bluster to be passed off as serious policy prescriptions.

Welcome to the asymmetric polarization of foreign policy. Even some of the basic terms of the debate are deceptive. For instance Republican often charge Democrats with abandoning the doctrine of American exceptionalism, a view of the United States as playing special role in upholding international rules and ideals. The idea of American exceptionalism is linked with the United States' proud history as a constitutional republic, the main author of global norms for the post-World War II world, and a pillar of the resulting international order. Contrary to the Republican talking points, this idea of a distinct U.S. global leadership role is still a core principle of mainstream Democratic thinking on foreign policy. Naturally Republicans want everyone to believe Democrats have moved to the left, because that would help hide the real asymmetry of the Republicans' own shift far to the right of center. We aren't debating whether America wears a mantle of leadership in world affairs; the controversy is really about the extra presumptions and arrogance that the far right has added on. More to the point, it is the Republicans who have adopted a radical concept of the U.S. global role: American omnipotence.

Is that too stark a characterization? It's true that no Republican would argue in so many words that the United States is all-powerful. Even so, the delusion of control over world events is the essence of contemporary GOP foreign policy thinking and the common thread of its prescriptions. Even if the right wing stops short of explicitly labeling America as almighty, their proposals give no hint of limits to America's sway.

The famous Rudy Giuliani quip that "hope is not a strategy" is ironically apt for his own party, which consistently peddles its foreign policy on the basis of best-case scenarios. Actually we can summarize some of the main assumptions, or blind spots, of GOP foreign policy in a few sentences:

First off, if the U.S. would simply ratchet up the pressure and project an image of strength, the government or group that we're pressuring will halt their problematic behavior. Moreover, there is no need to make concessions or accommodations in exchange. Nor is there any danger of pressure from the United States being undercut by other international players; after all, Republicans regularly remind us that America's allies desperately await our leadership. In civil wars, democratically oriented moderates would prevail if we provide military aid—but no need for U.S. boots on the ground—and be agents of reform once in power. When U.S. military power is demonstrated, the bad guys will respond by retreating rather than retaliating. As for America's moral authority, it is a given and doesn't require any steps on our part to maintain or replenish.

American omnipotence indeed seems like a more fitting label for this approach than exceptionalism, though American infallibility or narcissism might also be accurate. All the emphasis is on self-regard, with no effort at self-awareness or realistic consideration of the other players—particularly those players' options to reject the path we want them to take. When you hear all this bluster from the same party that promised Iraqis would greet U.S. forces as liberators, it's clear they didn't learn their lesson.

Philosophers have a term for the free will of those who act on their own accord: agency. This is the biggest blind spot of Republican foreign policy—the denial of others' agency. Their arguments make it sound like America is the world's only actor. In effect, everyone else is reduced to a non-entity and expected to comply with American wishes. The military has an adage cautioning against this very assumption: "the enemy gets a vote." An adult conversation about foreign policy and national security requires more realism about America's ability to affect the actions of others.

Keeping Things in Perspective

Despite the glaring superficiality of the right wing foreign policy approach, it still skews the debate on these issues in multiple ways—warping our judgment of success versus failure and our sense of proportion and priority. Overall, Republicans pull the focus of the debate toward the bad things that happen in and come from the Middle East. Given how much of the GOP's foreign policy pitch is aimed at stoking voters' fears, there is a certain cynical logic in trying to judge foreign policy effectiveness purely on the basis of events in that region. Then again, Republican electoral prospects might not be the proper gauge of success.

Even just looking at the issues Republicans push with regards to terrorism, it is not clear whether they are trying to discuss substance or just preening and trying to look tougher than Democrats. For all the times I have heard GOP politicians trumpet the label of "radical Islamic terrorism," they have never really explained the supposed crucial insight that goes with this label—how it offers a basis for a winning counterterrorism strategy. Rather than helping understand the nature of the threat, the point seems to be to maximize the sense of threat.

And what should we make of Republican proposals for new restrictions on immigrants and refugees, when the perpetrators of the terror attacks on U.S. soil have nearly all been American citizens? The attackers aren't coming into the country across our borders, they live here. Again, the agenda seems to be about the appearance of toughness rather than addressing the terrorist threat. In the process, the Republicans put themselves at odds with long traditions of religious freedom and protection of human rights. The debate over Syrian refugees lost sight of key facts, most important that the refugees are victims of ISIS who are vetted for a year or two before coming to the United States. The controversy also made it seem as if refugee resettlement in the U.S. is a special new initiative for Syrians, rather than what America has done for tens of thousands of persecution victims year in and year out. Where I live in Central Wisconsin, resettlement was how the local Hmong community originally got here from Laos two generations ago. It is the height of hypocrisy to preach freedom while slamming the door on refugees who left their countries because of repression. In fact, many of the Hmong and Iraqis resettled in the U.S. had been in danger back home because they had worked with American troops. The Syrian refugee debate represented a truly ugly political moment, with even some congressional Democrats who are otherwise progressive voting for the proposed restrictions.

None of which takes away from the seriousness of the terrorist threat or other challenges in the Middle East. There are important debates to be had about the different pieces of the counterterrorism puzzle: radicalization of homegrown terrorists; the use of drone strikes and the danger of spawning new terrorists; the residual U.S. military forces in Afghanistan and Iraq; the challenges of cooperating with key governments such as Pakistan and Saudi Arabia. Then there is the challenge of trying to fulfill the promise of Arab Spring and help ordinary Arabs gain the dignity and self-determination for which they so desperately yearn. Not to mention Sunni-Shia tensions in the region. Yet the bluster we hear from Republicans bears no resemblance to these substantive issues.

Besides, there are other problems with letting the discussion of foreign policy become consumed with hotspots like Syria. With hundreds of thousands of innocent lives lost, the war in Syria has been the world's greatest tragedy of the current period. For that reason alone, it is ripe for a discussion of whether our country has done its best to halt the carnage. But that discussion must be more honest than the

Republican fantasy of an almighty America—honest in reckoning with the tradeoffs, uncertainties, and difficulty for an outsider to overcome local forces and resolve a struggle for power in which they have much higher stakes than we. It is probably the trickiest military, diplomatic, and development challenge of all to try molding a stable political order after a country's power structure has been disrupted. Because of the tragic human toll in Syria, the search for solutions must continue. That does not mean, though, that Syria should be viewed as the United States' top foreign policy priority or as the prime test of success or failure.

In the bigger picture, America has much more of a stake in the political, security, and economic order of the international system as a whole. The top tier of the foreign policy agenda is comprised of challenges that, if allowed to worsen, could seriously erode the international system: keeping the global economy growing, stemming climate change, and checking the spread of nuclear weapons. The good news is that shoring up the international economic and security order, while hardly a walk in the park, is far less nettlesome than bringing peace to Syria. The better news is that President Obama leaves office having made significant progress on all three fronts—a diplomatic solution for the most urgent nuclear nonproliferation challenge, Iran, the global climate agreement reached in Paris, and cooperation with the world's other economic powers to pull out of the Great Recession. Crucially though, the key has been to exercise leadership by steadily bringing other players along, rather than issuing ultimatums. Back when she was Secretary of State, Hillary Clinton stressed this key point by saying that "part of leading is making sure you get other people on the field."

The remainder of this chapter will give more detailed contrasts between the Obama foreign policy record and the alternatives put forward by the opposition party. The issues that center on the Middle East (Iran's nuclear program and

Syria's civil war) have been hotly debated, in part because Republicans have highlighted that region. In both cases, the GOP critiques and proposals are based on wildly unrealistic and self-serving assumptions. Next we will review the strategic rationale for focusing on global systemic risks like climate change and nonproliferation, as opposed to conflict hotspots. When it comes to two other Obama administration priorities—the rebound of the global economy and the Paris climate deal—the Republicans' failures are sins of omission. These challenges simply aren't very high on their foreign policy agenda, climate change having apparently fallen off completely.

As in other chapters, the final sections will look back a few decades to remember a more sensible Republican Party and look ahead to sketch the outlines of a healthier right-left foreign policy debate. And in a further parallel with the last two chapters on the economy and healthcare reform, the Almighty America fallacy has led Republicans to misrepresent one of President Obama's major achievements as a failure.

Iran – Deal or No Deal?

The debate over President Obama's agreement with Iran to limit their nuclear program was a clear instance of asymmetric polarization—pitting the Republicans' pie-in-the-sky desirable outcome against the Obama administration's down-to-earth pursuit of an outcome that was actually attainable. In the run-up to the September 2015 congressional votes on the Iran deal, the opponents made bold claims about securing a "better deal" through continued sanctions and saber-rattling. But the reality was that after two years of negotiations and five years of sanctions, there was no possibility of a diplomatic solution on better terms. When critics claimed they could obtain better terms, those claims depended entirely on all the other players conveniently going along with their plan.

Presidential nominee Donald Trump voiced a standard GOP knock against the Iran Deal, phrased in his trademark clumsy syntax, when he characterized the deal as, "an agreement that will get them to nuclear quicker than [if] we had no agreement."[2] Yet judging by any reasonable or historical standard, the deal puts extremely stringent limits on the Iranian nuclear program and subjects it to highly intrusive verification, under penalty of re-imposed sanctions if Iran fails to comply. The verification measures and constraints on Iran's program are stricter than any agreement in arms control history. Instead of enriching uranium to the 20 percent purity that Iran previously had —way too close for comfort to weapons-grade—they are prohibited from enriching higher than 3.75 percent for 15 years. Meanwhile, their maximum allowable stockpile of low-enriched uranium is a token 300 kilograms, which required them to give up 98 percent of what they had. The way the enrichment process works is by running uranium through huge cascades of centrifuges. Iran previously operated nearly 20,000 centrifuges, yet for the next decade they'll have to mothball all but 6,104 of their least modern centrifuges, with strict limits on R&D that will constrain their ability to modernize afterwards. One result of these new constraints is to extend the breakout time it would take Iran to enrich enough uranium for a bomb—in the worst case that it made a sudden dash to the bomb— from 2-3 months previously to more than a year under the agreement.

To block Iran's other potential route to a bomb, by amassing plutonium, they will be prohibited for the next 15 years from reprocessing plutonium from their nuclear reactor waste (plus, the Iranians went even further by renouncing any intention of reprocessing in the longer term). And the U.S. and other international parties to the deal will know Iran's reactors intimately as they work alongside Iranians to redesign their main reactor and demolish a new plant that was under construction. Even more, the agreement ensures Iran's every move will be monitored not just for the operation of reactors and centrifuges, as in the past, but now also for related exports and imports as well as the mining of raw uranium.

Contrary to the picture painted by critics, some key provisions such as the mechanism for re-imposing sanctions (if needed) tilt heavily in favor of the U.S. In the process for handling disputes over compliance, a bloc vote of the U.S. and our European allies can rule against Iran without Russia or China's vote. If the dispute persists, the UN Security Council 'snap-back' process for sanctions is similarly rigged so the U.S. gets final say and China or Russia are kept from shielding Iran.

The Iran Deal was a case study in pragmatism—achieved by combining carrots and sticks, asserting American power without overplaying our hand, and forging a united front with a broad coalition of international partners. The only way to put the deal in a bad light is to conjure totally unrealistic alternatives. As we will see, the opposition's leading foreign policy spokespersons viewed the U.S. as holding all the cards, expected Iran to simply fold, sought a deal skewed completely in our favor, made blithe assumptions about the use of force, and counted on pliable international partners.

Let's start with a question Senator Marco Rubio raised in an article in the journal *Foreign Affairs.* After highlighting provisions of the deal such as continued uranium enrichment that he considered overly favorable for Iran, Rubio asked, "How did a nation with as little intrinsic leverage as Iran win so many concessions?"[3] The answer is very simple. Iran's leverage in the talks came from the technological progress it had made over the previous decade in mastering the nuclear fuel cycle, and their ability to keep getting nearer to a nuclear weapon capability.

The process leading to the Iran Deal had the same basic dynamic as any negotiation. Speaking as someone who actually took Negotiations 101 in graduate school, I can attest that the bargaining position of any party is a function of their ability to walk away and live with the status quo (it even has an acronym, BATNA, which stands for Best Alternative to a Negotiated Agreement). Since the point of these talks was to constrain Iran's nuclear activities, then a failure of the talks would leave Iran free to continue enriching uranium without new constraints. It's important to remember that the nuclear program stemmed from a determined national technical push for which the Iranian people endured considerable economic hardship, a price the outside world imposed for Iran's perseverance. Perhaps it might have been possible during the Bush administration to nip the enrichment effort in the bud, but by the mid-2010s the resulting capability was a hard-won technological achievement and a point of national pride. There was no chance Iran would willingly go back to square one. Having toughed it out for so long already, Iran would almost certainly continue to move closer to amassing ingredients for a potential weapon—again, the very source of international concern and Iranian leverage—rather than give up their whole program.

Of course the flip side of misreading and minimizing Iran's leverage, is to greatly overestimate America's. If you buy the illusion of an almighty America, Iran can be squeezed to make all the concessions without getting anything in return from the United States and the other negotiating parties. A reality-based foreign policy, though, recognizes the need for Iranian assent for a diplomatic solution. By the very definition of the word, an *agreement* depends on Iran agreeing to its provisions. Republican critics somehow imagine that constraints can be simply imposed on Iran. What they really want is a capitulation rather than an agreement. Typically, though, the only way to get a nation-state to capitulate is to militarily defeat and occupy that country, and no Republican of any stature proposed going that far. Nonetheless, Republicans did believe the mere threat of force would help reach a more favorable deal with Iran. As Senator Tom Cotton put it during the final few months of talks, "We need to reinvigorate the threat of use of force to drive our diplomacy. Diplomacy is always stronger when backed by credible threat of use of force."

The partisan divide on this issue is not whether diplomacy and the threat of force are complementary; most mainstream Democrats and Republicans would view that as basic statecraft. Where the parties differ is in the way they juxtapose diplomacy and force—it's the distinction between a) the prospect of eventual confrontation if diplomacy fizzles out and b) revving our engines for an attack right in the middle of a negotiation. In keeping with the principle that force should only be used as a last resort, President Obama saw the prospect of a nuclear-armed Iran as a threat that should be thwarted militarily if Iran failed to cooperate on a peaceful solution. Meanwhile his critics assumed that threatening an attack would soften Tehran's negotiating stance and discounted the possibility that it could undermine basic trust and goodwill.

For that matter, military action has dubious value as a way to deal with Iran's nuclear program. As has been widely recognized and noted, bombs cannot destroy the technical knowhow that a country's nuclear program is based on. The most that an attack on Iran's nuclear sites could accomplish is a temporary setback of the technological effort. According to two senior officers involved in planning such an attack, Iran could get back to where it was in as little as a year or two.[4] Given all the Republican outrage about key Iran Deal provisions expiring in 15 or 20 years, the much shorter-lasting impact of military strikes is important to keep in mind.

But the most ironic thing about the critics' position was

the hypocrisy of Republicans pushing for a credible threat of force while also objecting to Democrats framing the debate as a choice between diplomacy and war. Republicans wanted to rattle their sabers without being tagged as war mongers. They thought their policy of shunning a bad deal and military brinksmanship should be viewed as the surest path to a peaceful solution. There wouldn't be a war because Iran would give in. In other words, the Republicans were relying on Iran to relent. Which makes one wonder: exactly how does this count as a credible threat of force?

In all fairness, there was another element to the Republican claim of a false dichotomy of the existing deal versus going to war. Rather than calling for an immediate attack on Iran, Republicans advocated rejecting the deal, suspending the talks, and maintaining pressure through economic sanctions. Unfortunately this supposed alternative was in no way plausible. After all, these negotiations involved other parties besides the United States and Iran, and those other international players would be crucial for any further sanctions. Actually the question of whether they would help the United States move the goalposts of Iran diplomacy was not hypothetical. During congressional debate on the Iran deal, Senate Democratic Whip Dick Durbin invited colleagues to a briefing by ambassadors from those countries. The clear message: they weren't interested in pursuing a "better deal" after putting so much effort into reaching the July 2015 agreement. So when conservatives hoped to tighten—or even just maintain—multilateral sanctions for further pressure on Iran, it was pure fantasy.

In the end, there simply was not a better Iranian nuclear deal to be had. How can we be so sure in ruling out a counterfactual? Mainly because of the long and winding road that led to the Iran Deal. For all the right wing jabs at President Obama's supposed hunger for a deal and unwillingness to reject bad terms, early in his term the president did just that.

The key moment for tightened international sanctions came in 2010 after the Obama administration walked away from talks in which they saw Iranian backpedaling. For that matter, the process of reaching the final agreement in July 2015 reflected the administration's determination to get the best terms possible and came after two outline sets of understandings. In fact, Republicans spent months blasting Obama and Secretary of State John Kerry for extending the deadline of the talks while Sec. Kerry and the other American negotiators were pressing for some of the deal's toughest terms.

When the agreement was completed, it no longer mattered whether marginal improvements would have been possible. Practically speaking it was this deal or none at all, not just because the Iranians considered matters settled, but because the key global players involved did as well.

Middle East Morass

The most forthright stance on the Syrian civil war by an American political leader came from Hillary Clinton, and it was an expression of humility. As a presidential candidate, Clinton has acknowledged her past role in the Obama administration's internal debate on Syria but made a very soft-sell pitch for her alternative policy:

> I had a different strategy back when I was secretary of state, but I can't sit here today and tell you that if my strategy was followed we'd be in a different place because this has so much of a dynamic of its own.

The carnage in Syria and Northern Iraq is the most horrendous human tragedy in the world today. It has taken the lives of hundreds of thousands of ordinary Syrians and driven millions of others from their homes and communities, or from their country altogether. Meanwhile the bar-

baric Islamic State (or ISIS) spawned by the war has sunk to new depths of depravity, with their made-for-YouTube beheadings, and lured others such as the Paris, San Bernardino, Brussels, and Orlando attackers to their death cult. There's no disputing these grim realities—though we shouldn't exaggerate the ISIS threat to Americans—or the natural desire to stop the bloodshed.

For a reality-based policy debate about Syria and ISIS, though, we must clearly distinguish between taking action and achieving a desired result. Let the buyer beware of any Republican proposal for this region. Look very closely before letting it pass for a solution or even considering it ameliorative. More than likely, the Obama administration itself has already weighed the idea. Above all, watch out for glib assumptions about what the proposed step will achieve, the associated risks, or any special Republican powers to soften resistance through steely resolve.

When Secretary Clinton refers to "a dynamic of its own," it is a polite way of saying that the same factors that make the situation so horrific also make it extremely difficult to quell. The havoc in Syria is a function of the ruthlessness of the ruling Assad regime and its control of one of the strongest militaries in the region, both of which date back to Bashar al-Assad's father Hafez al-Assad. The military power, in turn, is the product of a longstanding relationship with Russia as its strategic client—an arrangement that is almost as important to Vladimir Putin because Russia's military bases in Syria help him try to stay relevant on the global stage. The Assad regime's other significant ally is the Islamic Republic of Iran, along with its terrorist subsidiary Hezbollah.

In other words, the Syrian crisis really deserves to be approached with a good measure of humility and prudence. For that matter, the same could be said Iraq itself, as well as Afghanistan and any country plagued with instability and violent power struggles. For a geographically remote outsider like the United States, to try remaking the power structure of another nation—let alone help it build a liberal political order with accountable governance—is among the hardest things to do.

Even some of the seemingly modest measures that have been debated are more complicated than they appear. It's naïve to assume, for instance, that humanitarian safe zones would keep us out of the fray. Our humanitarian intentions would run smack into the same violent realities they're meant to remedy. Any safe zone big enough to accommodate large numbers of people could become embroiled in the ongoing battle for control of territory. And even if safe zones could be set up, they could subsequently come under attack and/or be used as encampments for rebel forces. In other words, we shouldn't assume we would be greeted as neutral protectors; the safe zones idea could easily end up looking a lot like military involvement.

In fact, we know from a senior administration official's inside account that President Obama has pressed just these sorts of practical questions. Derek Chollet was involved in Syria policy in successive roles in the White House and Defense Department and summarized the president's approach this way:

> Describe for me specifically what will work, the president would demand, and if you can make a case we can get this done, we'll do it. Obama believed that while acting might provide short-term satisfaction, in the end it would do more harm than good.[5]

Providing military training to local forces is another popular idea among critics who want to do more in Syria. To highlight what an uncertain business this can be, Chollet quotes from an interview with Chairman of the Joint Chiefs of Staff Martin Dempsey, who did a previous stint with responsibility for training Iraqi forces. Gen. Dempsey told Greg Jaffe of the *Washington Post*, "Is it possible to build an indigenous force that will actually take control of its own destiny? I don't know."[6]

Meanwhile, one of Donald Trump's big applause lines on the campaign trail is his pledge to "knock the hell out of ISIS." Trump may not be aware that thousands of U.S. troops are in Iraq currently, helping local forces wrest towns and cities from ISIS control. They are deployed as part of a 60-nation coalition assembled to combat ISIS starting in 2014. In approximately two years, their air campaign has carried out over 11,000 airstrikes against more than 22,000 ISIS targets.[7]

Nor does Donald Trump have a monopoly on meaningless Republican tough talk, as shown by the following press statement from Sen. Ted Cruz in response to President Obama's December 2015 Oval Office address on ISIS:

> If I am elected President, I will direct the Department of Defense to destroy ISIS.

Mind you, a prepared statement issued by a sitting member of the Senate Armed Services Committee who was then seeking the presidency. It's hard to know even what to make of this. Perhaps some Republicans have repeated the mantra about following the advice of military commanders so often that they have forgotten the basics of civilian control of the military (we dealt with this in Al Franken's 2008 campaign). Contrary to Cruz's fantasy version of national security, new military action in Syria would require more engagement from a President Cruz than just giving the 'go' signal for a precooked surefire plan.

Perhaps it stems from asymmetric polarization. Republicans haven't been called out for their bullshit, and that has made it all too easy for them to coast on their image of toughness. Taking it for granted that their ideas would be taken seriously, they have basically stopped putting effort into actually making their proposals serious.

We're Really All in It Together

In keeping with his carefully built brand as his party's serious ideas guy, House Speaker Paul Ryan issued a series of working papers to lay out House Republicans' views on major policy issues. The paper on national security rendered the following verdict on President Obama: "American foreign policy is failing at nearly every turn. After eight years of broken promises, concessions, and retreat, America's adversaries sense weakness and are pressing their advantage around the globe." Has Obama foreign policy really been a string of failures, or do the president and the speaker have different agendas and therefore different definitions of success and failure?

The standard GOP knock against President Obama is that his policy has been feckless and abandoned America's global leadership role. But as discussed above, the Republican worldview tends to focus very narrowly on adversaries in one part of the world. The issue is not that the Obama administration has lacked a strategy. It did follow a strategy—one that Republicans didn't like and refused to acknowledge. The best encapsulation can be found in a couple passages from the 2015 version of the Obama administration's National Security Strategy. The first is taken from a list of enduring U.S. national interests that had also been used by the administration to frame the 2010 version of the strategy. The second describes the kind of effort needed to advance that interest:

- A rules-based international order advanced by U.S. leadership that promotes peace, security, and opportunity through stronger cooperation to meet global challenges.

In an interconnected world, there are no global problems

that can be solved without the United States, and few that can be solved by the United States alone. American leadership remains essential for mobilizing collective action to address global risks and seize strategic opportunities. Our closest partners and allies will remain the cornerstone of our international engagement. Yet, we will continuously expand the scope of cooperation to encompass other state partners, non-state and private actors, and international institutions—particularly the United Nations, international financial institutions, and key regional organizations. These partnerships can deliver essential capacity to share the burdens of maintaining global security and prosperity and to uphold the norms that govern responsible international behavior.

Let me translate from the original wonkspeak. American exceptionalism is not an individual sport and entails a great deal of international teamwork. Responding effectively to our most urgent challenges is a matter of making sure other key players join together with us and that everyone does part. Even though America's friends and allies are crucial, relying solely on like-minded nations will not be enough to deal with some of the problems we face. Fortunately, most of the world's influential nations have a shared interest in addressing those problems.

The United States has a huge stake in whether the 21st-century world is shaped by disintegration and disorder or by the social contract of a rules-based international order. This stake is especially high for the world's most powerful nation, but others are likely to be pulled upward or downward along the same trajectory—either rising standards of living and relative tranquility, or ruthless power struggles, exploitation and abuse. For a reminder of the importance having of a basic social contract, just think back to 2008 when the global financial system nearly came completely unraveled. Markets came dangerously close to the financial version of a Hobbesian "war of all against all." Large Wall Street firms were revealed to be intensely interdependent and vulnerable to the gaps in one another's balance sheets. The very solidity of the system—the mutual trust and confidence that participants rely on to function—was under threat from a mad scramble of self-help.

Fortunately we managed to pull back from that precipice, and I'm not suggesting that the world is pervasively nasty and brutish. The point is rather that it will take effort, political will, and international cooperation to ward off that kind of danger. And it's not hard to see why most nations share an interest in tackling these problems. All you need to do is imagine the consequences of failure. A world with a stagnant global economy, a 4-5°F temperature rise, and/or 15-20 nuclear-armed nations would be bad for everyone. As interconnected as the world has become, to say that we're all in it together isn't a declaration of idealism but a statement of fact.

Back in 2005, then Deputy Secretary of State Robert Zoellick gave a synopsis of this shared interest that holds up quite well more than a decade later. In a major speech on U.S.-China relations, Zoellick coined the term responsible stakeholder:

> All nations conduct diplomacy to promote their national interests. Responsible stakeholders go further: They recognize that the international system sustains their peaceful prosperity, so they work to sustain that system. In its foreign policy, China has many opportunities to be a responsible stakeholder.

Zoellick's idea explains why it is vital, and not merely a charitable act, for key nations to contribute to the global greater good. And it underscores the need to prioritize those contributions in U.S. foreign policy as a whole and relations with China in particular. In other words, what the National Security Strategy said about the U.S. also goes for China: there are few if any global problems that can be solved without its help.

The U.S.-China relationship is a mixture of competition and cooperation, yet the tensions are usually played up more than the collaboration is, something I've observed at conferences and meetings with other foreign policy specialists. Time after time I would hear colleagues confidently predict that China would stand firm on its narrow selfish interests. Beijing would never help pressure Iran, reduce greenhouse gases, or rebalance the global economy. Until, that is, they relented and did all of those things. Sometimes these skeptics fall behind the times. In a bipartisan discussion of U.S. grand strategy, I heard one conservative national security expert say China wouldn't rebalance their economy from exports toward domestic consumption, even though such a shift was already incorporated into the last version of China's five-year economic plan.

For much of his presidency, the top item on President Obama's domestic and foreign policy agenda were one and the same: avoiding a repeat of the Great Depression and recovering from the Great Recession. The political fault lines were similar in the domestic and international arenas too—with supply-siders pushing for austerity and demand-siders calling for stimulus.

The financial crisis reached its terrifying climax in late-2008 and early-2009, during the waning months of the Bush administration and President Obama's first months in office. In the most acute phase of the crisis, Republicans in Congress were the "Austerian" outliers; there was an overwhelming consensus among other players on the need for government intervention in the economy. In fact, the outgoing and incoming presidential administrations had a very smooth handoff and substantial continuity. It was the Bush administration that set up the crucial TARP program to help financial institutions start lending again, and they also made the initial moves to rescue the auto industry.

At the international level President Bush launched a new summit-level venue for stewardship of the global economy, the G20, which President Obama solidified as an ongoing process of economic cooperation. By April 2009 the G20 nations marshaled a combined $5 trillion of fiscal stimulus from their government budgets and guaranteed an additional $1 trillion in credit via the International Monetary Fund for governments needing to borrow. The next year, though, differences between Obama and his Austerian counterparts led to an open split at the G20's June 2010 summit in Toronto. Worried that the recovery wasn't yet strong enough to dial back deficit spending, Obama sent his colleagues a pre-summit letter urging against a premature shift from stimulus to deficit-reduction. Nonetheless he was rebuffed by the advocates of austerity, principally British Prime Minister David Cameron and German Chancellor Angela Merkel.

This split with our European allies (as well as Canadian Prime Minister Stephen Harper) bears a couple lessons. The first regards substance, recalling once again that the facts were on the side of Obama and demand-side / middle-out economics. America's recovery has been more robust than those of both Britain, which slipped back into recession, and Germany. As already noted, our federal deficit came down as a result of a stronger economy rather than budget cuts. And to have such a family spat within the like-minded Western countries is itself noteworthy. Think about it, on the biggest challenge facing the world in the late-2000s and early-2010s, the United States was divided from some of its closest allies. Not that disagreement among allies is inherently a problem. The real problem is with the idea—a frequent talking point on the right—that standing shoulder-to-shoulder with our allies is the answer for all major foreign policy challenges.

As much as Republicans like making all issues into a fight between the good guys and bad guys, that isn't a very useful guide in the real world.

When the Obama National Security Strategy talked about "expand[ing] the scope of cooperation" it was an oblique way of noting an important feature of the 21st-century world: that international politics are becoming more fluid, with dividing lines and coalitions that will shift depending on the issue. It's the global version of the old saying about politics and strange bedfellows.

Tragedy of the Commons

The challenge of eliciting contributions toward the greater good is familiar territory for political scientists, who use the term *collective action problem* or hearken back to the so-called tragedy of the commons first described in the early-19th century. In pre-industrial revolution Britain, common grazing grounds were vulnerable to being depleted unless local cattle owners took care to manage the combined grazing of their herds. Two centuries later, global warming represents the ultimate potential tragedy of the commons. The severity of climate change depends on the combined volume of greenhouse gases we human beings put into the atmosphere; if we want to keep the global temperature rise from being catastrophic, we have no choice but to work our way toward low-carbon economies as quickly as possible. So as a policy and diplomatic matter, getting every nation to do its part is a rather large collective action problem.

In a perverse way, Republicans were counting on China's intransigence for a key piece of their climate change position. The GOP has a multi-layered argument against trying to limit carbon emissions (Snowballs! Lightbulbs!). One layer has been a variation on "after you, my dear Alphonse" that says the United States shouldn't have to limit our emissions while

China and India refuse to do likewise. On closer inspection, it is interesting to hear this argument from Republicans because it assumes a link between the standard of behavior for the United States and other countries—something the right wing is generally uncomfortable with. Even more problematic for conservatives, leaders in China and India ultimately yielded to demands that they act like responsible stakeholders, making it harder for Republicans to hide behind them.

In terms of the diplomatic landmarks of climate action, most of President Obama's tenure is bracketed by high-profile UN climate summits in Copenhagen in December 2009 and Paris in December 2015, where the first truly global climate agreement was reached. The Copenhagen meeting got a very bad rap as a purported debacle. While it's true that the discussions were chaotic and badly organized—agreement was only reached when President Obama barged in on a meeting among the leaders of China, India, Brazil, and South Africa—they also fell victim to unrealistic expectations. There was no way the conference could live up to its hype as a do-or-die moment. Much more time was needed to develop workable frameworks and compromises.

In fact, the broad principles that were agreed at Copenhagen should be considered an important precursor for the Paris Agreement. Recall that the previous global climate accord, the Kyoto Protocol, allowed the greenhouse gas emissions of major emerging economies such as China and India to grow rather than requiring reductions. Given that China's share of annual global CO_2 emissions grew from 16 percent to over 25 percent in the last decade, and India has emerged as the world's third largest emitter, this was a huge flaw. But in Copenhagen both countries made their first-ever commitments to limit emissions, promising to reduce the carbon-intensity of their economic growth so that their emissions would grow at a slower rate than their economies. To build momentum for Paris, Chinese President Xi Jinping and

President Obama in November 2014 announced a bilateral agreement in which China went even further: pledging that by 2030 China's annual emissions would stop growing and start tapering off.

Copenhagen also established the basic framework for how a global climate deal would work, a pledge-and-review system whereby each nation would declare its own emissions commitment—with accounting and verifications measures to gauge everyone's performance. The key idea, in diploma-tese, was intended nationally determined contributions (IN-DCs). This voluntary system was criticized by some purists who yearned for a top-down regime, with the world commu-nity imposing compulsory constraints on the biggest pollut-ers. According to the critique, world leaders lack the political will for the kind of ambitious boldness necessary in order to check global warming.

Yet I have argued that the problem is uncertainty rather than political will. What leaders need is a clearer sense of the ramifications of climate action. They need to know the im-pact of the different climate measures they could adopt—on their economies as well as on the level of greenhouse gases in the atmosphere.[8] Critics look at the Paris Agreement as setting a ceiling level for ambition, when we should really view it as a floor. By starting with these INDCs, governments will find out what works best to reduce greenhouse gases and thus gain the confidence to make more stringent commit-ments. This is the same progression from weaker to stronger multilateral regimes that's worked for other spheres such as arms control, human rights, and G20 cooperation on bal-anced economic growth.[9]

Another important contrast between the Republican and Democratic foreign policy approaches is their very dif-ferent concepts of moral authority. Republicans tend to view moral authority as somehow inherent to the United States. Maybe after hearing the mantra of "leader of the free world" so many times, they believe their own press. At any rate, Infallible America seems to be a corollary of the Almighty America doctrine. Most Democrats, on the other hand, realize that moral authority must be actively maintained rather than just presumed or baldly asserted.

A key example of the need for the United States to walk the walk was the 2010 U.S.-Russian New START agreement. If the U.S. wanted to press Iran to abide by their Nonproliferation Treaty (NPT) obligation and keep their nuclear activities civilian, then we had to make good on our NPT obligation to reduce our nuclear arsenal. Republicans scoffed at the idea that U.S. nuclear arms cuts would tug at the consciences of Iranian leaders, but in their smug assumptions about American moral superiority, the skeptics completely missed the point. It wasn't a question of earning the Iranian regime's admiration as a role model, but ostracizing them and painting their actions as contrary to membership in good standing in the world community. Think of it as the moral authority of the other guy looking like a jerk. America couldn't isolate Iran on our own. The U.S. needed the support of the rest of the world, support that depended on America also doing its part to uphold the NPT.

Republicans Didn't Always Think Treaties Gave You Cooties

Speaking of moral paragons, wounded World War II veteran and former Republican Senate Leader Bob Dole returned to the Senate floor in December 2012 —wheelchair-bound and together with spouse / former Senator Elizabeth Dole—to press for ratification of the Convention on the Rights of Persons With Disabilities (CRPD). Yet the allergy today's Republicans have against international obligations is so virulent that 38 of them spurned the Doles and blocked ratification.

What made the episode truly absurd was nature of the agreement on which they were voting. The essence of the disability rights convention is to spur other nations to emulate the U.S. Congress' own 1990 Americans With Disabilities Act. The administration of another World War II vet (and Republican), President George H.W. Bush, negotiated the agreement in order to establish American protections of disabled rights as the global standard. Yet somehow four out of five Senate Republicans voted against having the United States join 126 other nations that had already ratified the treaty.

In the ratification debate, opponents voiced their disdain for international agreements. A great example came from Senator Jon Kyl of Arizona, who objected that...

> I don't believe that we need to ratify an international convention to demonstrate our firm commitment in this area. Just as with many treaties before this one, the CRPD would offer cover to regimes that have no intention of actually helping their citizens.

So in his view, this accord was nothing but a charade that would help rogue governments bask in an aura of virtue. But what about using other governments' official commitments to international standards to hold them to account? If this is all just a cynical game, then logically it follows that we can't ever use rogue regimes' treaty obligations against them. After all, we never believed their sincerity in the first place.

What a long strange trip it's been from the middle of the last century to the first couple decades of this one. After the Second World War, American statesmen of that era (mostly men, but also Eleanor Roosevelt) worked to codify sets of international norms as the standards for any nation to be considered a pillar the world community. The standards even ensnared the United States itself—as America's Cold War adversaries highlighted our racial discrimination and gave added outside pressure for the protection of black Americans' rights. But Sen. Kyl seemed to say America doesn't need treaties to tell right from wrong, overlooking the fact that signed agreements give a lot more leverage on the behavior of other governments than just the superpower's say-so.

Another example of Republicans' rightward shift on international affairs was mentioned briefly at the beginning of this chapter: a fading shadow of John McCain's sensible moderation. Sen. McCain had plenty of reasons to show interest in U.S. ratification of the Comprehensive Test Ban Treaty (CTBT), as he did in 2007. Test detonations of nuclear weapons are lagging indicators of proliferation. When a country conducts an initial nuclear test, that event signals its official debut as a nuclear-armed power. After that, the proverbial horse is out of the barn. It is wise, therefore, to have a global prohibition of tests to keep nations from crossing that threshold—which is exactly the purpose of the CTBT, another agreement that was concluded by the Bush 41 administration.

Meanwhile the United States conducted so many tests during our first 47 years as a nuclear power (1,030 to be exact) that we have now refrained from further detonations for more than two decades under a self-imposed moratorium. The extensive earlier testing gave the U.S. all the technical insight on nuclear warheads we will ever need. A good time, in other words, to block others from climbing the n-weapon learning curve. But the substantive merits of the CTBT are one thing, and the politics are another. In 1999 a major opportunity was lost when the Senate voted against ratification of the treaty, then still relatively young. Senator McCain's interest in revisiting the issue was a testament to the agreement's value. His abandonment of the idea stemmed from the lack of any similar interest among his Republican colleagues.

These examples are snap-shot views of a Republican party growing increasingly hostile toward international agreements and any notion of a U.S. responsibility to abide by certain norms. But there is a longitudinal data set that shows the trend as well. Throughout the nuclear age, the arsenals of the United States and Russia (formerly the Soviet Union) have comprised the great majority of the world's nuclear weapons, and since the early 1970s the two nations have negotiated a series of treaties limiting the size and composition of those arsenals. From 1972-2010 the U.S. Senate voted to ratify five bilateral agreements on U.S. and Russian / Soviet strategic (long-range) forces. For all but the most recent ratification vote—in 1972, 1992, 1996, 2003—the vote was overwhelming, never with fewer than 87 in support and a maximum of six opponents. Then came a vote that exceeded the minimum needed for ratification by just four senators: approval of President Obama's 2010 New START agreement by a margin of 71-26.

The aforementioned Arizona Sen. Jon Kyl also figures prominently in this story. Sen. Kyl had long been active and vocal on arms control issues and positioned himself as a swing vote whose cue would be followed by many Republican colleagues. The Obama administration courted Kyl assiduously and offered, as a sweetener, robust funding that Kyl wanted for updates to the nuclear arsenal's technical infrastructure. For all the times President Obama has been slammed for supposedly getting rooked by international players, this was truly an instance of a rotten deal. If Kyl had bargained in good faith and supported New START, the margin for its ratification would probably have been much closer to the historical average.

As a matter of institutional norms and traditions, it's worth noting that a number of the Republicans who voted 'yes' were members of the Senate Foreign Relations Committee. Meanwhile we should also note the Committee's key role in ultimately putting the Iran Deal into effect. Senate Foreign Relations Chair Bob Corker worked with the Obama administration to devise a process that gave Republicans a chance to vote against the Iran Deal without derailing it. Not full-scale bipartisan cooperation perhaps, but absolutely critical nonetheless.

Returning to the ratification of New START, my favorite statement in the debate came from Senator Lamar Alexander, a member of the Republican leadership. Sen. Alexander said he supported New START because the agreement "leaves our country with enough nuclear warheads to blow any attacker to Kingdom come." That pretty much says it. As long as the U.S. retains an ability to retaliate and therefore deter a nuclear attack on us or our allies, the rest is just political posturing.

Toward a More Constructive Debate

In world affairs, the relationship between politics and policy is complicated. There is a taboo against letting politics shape foreign policy, even though domestic policy has no analogous rule. Commentators and historians remind us regularly that the quaint idea of politics stopping at the water's edge has always been just that, quaint. Yet the norm of setting politics aside endures. Participants in the foreign policy debate sometimes charge opponents with politicizing national security—which is just a different way of saying the same thing. (And no behind-the-scenes account of statecraft would be complete without the president at some point telling his aides to 'let me worry about the politics.') All of which seems to imply that judicious policy and political luster pull in opposite directions, though there's no intrinsic reason they should. Political sensitivity is an overlay on the substance of an issue; it isn't inherent in the policy options themselves. Politics has its own imperatives and affects any policy decisions where political combatants see a chance for controversy and advantage.

The corollary of the above critique of the national security discourse is that there is a more constructive debate we could be having—that it's possible for the perspectives of the right and left to be in creative tension and together shape sensible policy. In the Iran Deal case, for instance, some advocates for a tough deal contributed ideas that led to a strengthened agreement. As discussed above, the real political problem was the fire-breathers who were bound to view any agreement with Iran as the end of the world. The most hotly contested debate, therefore, wasn't about the fine points of the Joint Comprehensive Plan of Action but the question of whether the U.S. and the world are better off with an agreement or without.

The same differentiation between levels of discourse goes for any matter of policy. Most of the deep-in-the-weeds details are left to technical experts. (In a way, that is the very definition of political sensitivity, issues that are 'above the pay grade' of technical experts.) At the other extreme are the hot-button issues that are fodder for cable news, talk radio, blogs, editorial pages, and other commentary. But if we're looking for an optimal interplay between politics and substance, sometimes there can be discussion of sensitive issues without all the shouting. This is the sort of discourse that truly produces more light than heat.

For all the reasons outlined above, it is not easy to find topics that could lend themselves to a healthier debate. One possibility comes from a former senior adviser to Sen. John McCain and signatory to the Republican foreign policy establishment's Never-Trump pledge. The issue is related to President Obama's risk-averse approach. As noted by Derek Chollet, Obama consistently kept sight of the potential downside of an intensive military or diplomatic commitment to a given issue or crisis. Sometimes a president says, in effect, 'I have worried about the domestic and international politics of the matter, as well as the chances of success versus unintended consequences, and I don't like the odds.'

When I was in graduate school I took a class with Prof. Richard Neustadt, one of the country's most eminent students of the presidency. The central point of Neustadt's classic text *Presidential Power and the Modern Presidents* was about the loneliness of the office and what it means for presidents' decisions. While a president can gather up a great deal of information and analysis from advisers and other officials, no one other than s/he—not even the most loyal of loyalists—is in a position to judge what is best for him/her. Prof. Neustadt's theory came to mind when President Obama famously told reporters on Air Force One that his policy motto was "don't do stupid shit," basically highlighting the hazards of the do-something reflex and the underappreciated value of simply avoiding creating messes. As Prof. Neustadt might observe, the reporters are mainly interested in having foreign policy action to write about and don't have the same stake in success or failure as the president.

As with anything else, though, even an impulse that is mainly quite reasonable can be taken too far. There can be such a thing as an overabundance of caution. Which brings us to my pick for Most Constructive Foreign Policy Critique By a Republican: Richard Fontaine's essay for *Politico Magazine* "Obama's 'Slippery Slope' Delusion." The former McCain adviser and current president of the bipartisan think tank Center for a New American Security focused his January 2016 *Politico* piece on President Obama's approach to the use of military force. In a departure from the usual Republican slam, Fontaine observes that Obama has been remarkably willing to use force. The real problem is the way Obama has tried to curtail those military commitments—always so leery of "the inexorable escalation that might accompany the employment of force" (aka slippery slope) that he publicly renounces certain options that he ends up pursuing later.

Fontaine drives home the ramifications with the following counterfactual:

> Imagine, for a moment, the opposite approach. Imagine if instead of pledging all of the things America would not do at the beginning of the fight against the Islamic State, Obama instead announced everything he has authorized since. If in initiating hostilities the president said he would send 3,500 American troops back to Iraq; supply weapons to Kurds, Sunni tribes in western Iraq, and the Iraqi security forces; conduct an extensive anti-ISIL bombing campaign across Iraq and Syria; provide close air support for Iraqi units retaking portions of Anbar province; deploy special operations forces to Syria; arm thousands of fighters in Syria willing to take on the Islamic State; share intelligence with local ground units; and send special operations units to kill or capture key ISIL leaders—had he announced all this, his plans would have been seen as a major attempt to wrest momentum from the Islamic State.
>
> Instead, his administration has done all of these things piecemeal. The collective effect has been diluted by the incremental escalation and the insistence that this time, really, represents all the president is willing to do.[10]

Fair enough. And I can see related problems for other cases where the argument for using force was compelling. For the 2011 intervention in Libya, worries about a slippery slope led Obama to differentiate sharply between the missions of protecting the people of Eastern Libya against massacre versus removing Muammar Gaddafi from power. Technically there is indeed a difference; if Gaddafi could have been deterred from slaughtering his own people, then policy change without regime change would be the goal. On the other hand, what if Gaddafi was bound and determined to slaughter the people of Benghazi and other towns, then wouldn't regime change be integral to the humanitarian mission? Indeed it turned out that removing the Libyan dictator was necessary to keep him from committing mass atrocities. From accounts of the private UN Security Council deliberations, this possibility was thoroughly discussed. Still, Fontaine makes a fair critique of Obama's public renunciation of regime change.

To his credit, Fontaine takes pains to acknowledge that military commitments can be prone to underestimation and expansion—that some slopes are slippery. Even so, the way he categorizes certain scenarios as either plausible or paranoid is debatable. Count me skeptical, for instance, that "had the administration developed a plan for securing Libya after Qadhafi's overthrow, it may have avoided the conversion of that country into a chaotic safe haven for international terrorism." Somehow I think it would have been harder than it sounds.

But that's the point, isn't it, for progressives and conservatives to debate these questions in the service of an effective foreign policy. If we are trying to rediscover the midfield of the foreign policy debate—between the proverbial 40-yard lines—then Fontaine's guidelines for right-sizing military commitments offer some useful terms for such a debate.

Further Reading

Chollet, Derek. *The Long Game: How Obama Defied Washington and Redefined America's Role in the World.* New York: Public Affairs Books, 2016.

Hachigian, Nina and David Shorr. "The Responsibility Doctrine." *The Washington Quarterly*, Winter 2013.

Jones, Bruce. *Still Ours to Lead: America, Rising Powers, and the Tension Between Rivalry and Restraint.* Washington: Brookings Institution Press, 2014.

Mann, James. *The Obamians: The Struggle Inside the White House to Redefine American Power.* New York: Viking, 2012.

Rothkopf, David. *National Insecurity: American Leadership in an Age of Fear.* New York: Public Affairs Books, 2014.

Weber, Steven and Bruce W. Jentleson. *The End of Arrogance: America in the Global Competition of Ideas.* Cambridge, MA: Harvard University Press, 2010.

5

Fraudulent Voters

While the other three fallacies in our quartet were linked to spheres of public policy, the last of the set focuses on one of the fundamentals of democratic governance: the proverbial ballot box. This puts us in the realm of America's civil religion. The image of America as a paragon of popular self-government is central to our national identity. It is a matter of firm principle that every citizen has an equal say in determining our destiny as a society.

The ballot box is the tool we use to allocate political power. So in the interest of a fair playing field, the process and rules for elections should be beyond the realm of politics. Campaigns and legislative debates are political contests by nature, but the process of conducting elections should be neutral ground and purely technical. By and large, the dictates of fairness are not debatable. We all understand what constitutes fair play and faithfulness to democratic ideals.

Especially for a nation that evangelizes about self-government and free and fair elections to others around the world—

and which had our own wrenching history of extending the franchise, gradually and after violent battles—it ought to be a clear-cut imperative for citizens to have the fullest practical opportunity to vote. Conservatives regularly lecture us about upholding the ideals on which America was founded; surely it must be a core value to encourage all Americans to take part in our elections.

Which brings us to the question of how we find ourselves in a partisan fight over restrictions on Americans' ability to vote? The short answer is that Republicans have concocted a cover story to pretend the debate is about something else— namely, so-called voter fraud. For the reasons just outlined, Republicans are constrained by the norms of polite society from openly talking about keeping people from voting. So for them, the myth of voters using false identities to tilt elections is a crucial pretext for a variety of measures whose effect (and real purpose) is to make it harder to vote. With so much deceit, the debate about voter suppression often has an upside down Alice in Wonderland quality. Most corrosive of all: the travesty by which conjured-out-of-thin-air bogeymen, the fraudulent voters, serve as the grounds for arbitrarily curtailing the rights of large numbers of actual Americans.

Yet in a strange way, the outright dishonesty of Republican voting suppression efforts also points the way out of this mess. As time goes on, the truth of the matter is bound to emerge; the facts are just too clear to ignore. This chapter will examine the political strategy hidden by the Republicans' cover story, the Bush administration's witch hunt for prosecution of fraud, and how that effort blurred the line between so-called voting integrity and voter intimidation / suppression. Then we will look at why voter fraud is a terrible technique for stealing an election and how this reality led judges to stretch and strain in order to uphold voter ID laws. Next I'll offer a battlefront report from here in Wisconsin, including my own April 2016 city council election. Then the chapter will conclude in the same way as the others, reviewing the history of a Republican Party that was more supportive of voting rights and looking toward the constructive debate we could have if the GOP swung back toward the middle.

For all their discipline in sticking to the cover story, occasionally Republicans themselves blurt the truth in moments of unintended candor or as conscientious whistleblowers. We begin with one of the founding fathers of movement conservatism in the 1970s: Paul Weyrich. In addition to founding the infamous American Legislative Exchange Council (ALEC), Weyrich was involved in launching many of the right wing's other key institutions—Heritage Foundation, Moral Majority, and Free Congress Foundation, to name just a few. Thanks to a progressive group that serves as a watchdog over the far-right, People for the American Way, we can look back at an archived 1980 video clip of Weyrich summing up the political strategy behind voter suppression decades before the Republicans' recent wave of voter ID laws:

> I don't want everybody to vote. Elections are not won by a majority of people. They never have been from the beginning of our country, and they are not now. As a matter of fact our leverage in the elections quite candidly goes up as the voting populace goes down.

The statement is impressive in its frankness, if nothing else. Without mincing words, Weyrich told fellow conservatives that their best strategy for putting a thumb on the electoral scale was to limit the size of the electorate. As a purely practical matter, the strategy is certainly less arduous than vying for voters' support on the strength of conservative ideas and candidates. Then again, this kind of gaming of the system basically tries to bypass the popular mandate that is supposed to be the basis of legitimacy in public office. Enacting restrictions on voting puts Republicans in ethically dubious territory and represents a test of conscience for their party.

At the very moment I am writing this chapter, the voter ID law here in Wisconsin is literally on trial in US District Court. The One Wisconsin Institute and Citizen Action of Wisconsin Education Fund sued the state's Government Accountability Board to remove barriers that Republicans enacted to make it harder—especially for African-Americans, Latinos, and other Democrat-leaning constituencies—to register and vote. Later in the chapter, there will be more discussion of the different voting suppression tactics cited in the Wisconsin case and others. Meanwhile this case offers a rare glimpse into the debate among Republican state legislators themselves.

Because a few conscientious legislators flinched at the attempt to rig the system, we got a behind-the-scenes glimpse of internal Republican squabbles. For instance the original complaint filed by the plaintiffs in 2015 quoted a public objection by former Republican State Senator Dale Schultz, who left the senate the previous year:

> [W]e should be pitching as political parties our ideas for improving things in the future rather than mucking around in the mechanics and making it more confrontational at our voting sites and trying to suppress the vote.

Schultz's mention of confrontations at the polls is likely a reference to revised rules enabling election observers to stand as close as three feet from election workers as they check voters in. We should note that the most aggressive election observers—those particularly eager to be as close as possible—are basically vigilantes who are infamous for scrutinizing black and Latino voters.

When *One Wisconsin vs. Judge Nichol et al* recently went to trial, a former aide to Sen. Schultz pulled back the curtain even farther and disclosed what legislators said about voter ID in private. The former staffer, Todd Allbaugh, quoted then-Senator Glenn Grothman saying "What I'm concerned about here is winning, and that's what really matters here. ... We better get this done quickly while we have the opportunity." After Allbaugh began posting on Facebook about the internal Republican debate, he was contacted by Grothman from the latter's new perch in the U.S. House of Representatives. In their last exchange Congressman Grothman said "Well, here's the thing ... I fundamentally believe Democrats cheat, OK? I do. And I don't believe our side does."

The congressman is hardly the only Republican to believe in the fraudulent Democratic voter as an article of faith. In fact, the last Republican presidential administration was quite zealous about cracking down on voter fraud—going as far as an attempt to enlist federal law enforcement in their electoral strategy. The scandal reached a climax after a politically motivated set of firings of nine US attorneys in 2006, with prosecution of voter fraud as one of the motives. Yet its origins were rooted in the 2000 election.

Aftershocks of the 2000 Election

Florida's famously re-tabulated and litigated presidential vote was one of several nail-biters that November. After all the results were official, Al Gore's margin in New Mexico was the narrowest in the union at a mere 366 votes. Later when the scandal erupted, the local US attorney fired by the Bush White House was a central figure, particularly in connection with the crackdown on voter fraud.

The Missouri race for US Senate was where the ball got rolling. Just 19 days before Election Day, Democratic challenger and then-Governor Mel Carnahan was killed in a plane crash. By then it was too late to change the ballots, so Missouri's new governor pledged to appoint his predecessor's widow, Jean Carnahan, to the senate seat if her late husband received the most votes. Sure enough, Republican incumbent Senator John Ashcroft lost to the deceased governor and immediately lashed out with vague charges about fraud in St. Louis. (Urban centers with sizable black and Hispanic populations are always Republican targets for such charges, which are dog whistles or rallying cries depending on whether you consider them to be at all subtle.) Other top Missouri Republican officials such as Ashcroft's colleague Senator Kit Bond and then-Secretary of State Matt Blunt filled in some of the details in the months after the election, based on investigations by their staff. I should immediately add that the terms details and investigation are used here very loosely, because the charges of fraud quickly crumbled under closer examination—as they so often do. After releasing his 51-page report on "Election Turmoil in St. Louis," Blunt was forced to walk back his allegations of multiple voting, convicted felon voters, voting from addresses that were supposedly empty lots, and unqualified election judges who themselves were not registered to vote. The numbers in Blunt's report under these headings didn't hold up due to inaccurate government records, names matched to the wrong people, flawed assumptions, and the overall sloppiness of a politically motivated witch hunt.

Ashcroft decided against pressing the matter in his own election; the 49,000-vote margin was too large to overcome with a recount. But in his excellent history, *Give Us the Ballot*, Ari Berman captured the lasting import of the 2000 Missouri senate race: "Less than two months later, Bush nominated Ashcroft as attorney general, and a new right-wing voter fraud movement was born."[1] Upon taking office as the country's new top law enforcement official, Ashcroft pushed St. Louis-style cheating (purported) toward the top of his agenda and launched a new Voting Access and Integrity Initiative. For future elections, the Department of Justice (DoJ) would serve as watchdogs—poised to help with any problems on the ground anywhere around the country. Besides the department's national hotline, all of its regional US Attorneys' offices had expert prosecutors designated as contact points. Special seminars were held for Justice Department lawyers to ensure they were well versed in election law.

In keeping with the initiative's name, a 2002 fact sheet outlining DoJ efforts for that year's midterm elections took pains to emphasize their both sides of its dual-mandate:

- The Department of Justice has responsibility for enforcing the laws guaranteeing voting rights and prosecuting voting fraud. The Civil Rights and Criminal divisions of the Department of Justice are involved in elections to ensure both ballot access and ballot integrity.

  >The Civil Rights Division is charged with enforcing the Voting Rights Act of 1965 as well as the National Voter Registration Act, both of which are designed to guarantee access to the polls on Election Day.

  >The Criminal Division is responsible for enforcing the voting fraud laws passed by Congress and signed by the President.

It was a message meant to reassure Americans that federal law enforcement would help thwart illegal votes while staunchly upholding the rights of all qualified voters, so that no one was deprived of their franchise. Unfortunately, though, measures aimed at the former problem tend to aggravate the latter one. As the shoddy 2001 Missouri Secretary of State report demonstrated, the grounds for disqualifying voters should be handled with great care. The errors in that report showed how qualified voters can get ensnared in the hunt for fraud—how easy it is for ballot integrity 'solutions' to become ballot access obstacles.

This is no mere theoretical possibility, as civil rights groups know from bitter experience. Soon after the announcement of Ashcroft's initiative, the Leadership Conference on Civil Rights (LCCR) joined with 23 other groups to express their concerns in a letter to the Attorney General:

> It has long been the experience of the civil rights community that overly aggressive "voting integrity" efforts, instead of reducing fraud, tend to intimidate lawful voters and ultimately suppress voter turnout. This is especially true when investigations and prosecutions appear to concentrate efforts on or target voters of a particular racial, ethnic, disability or other minority group…
>
> [W]e are deeply concerned about the resources dedicated to this federal-led investigation and the manner in which it has been conducted. While state authorities are normally called upon to investigate most types of election fraud, the involvement of considerable FBI resources and personnel has unnecessarily raised the profile of the investigation and has led to false perceptions among the public that "massive" fraud has been taking place. Even if such investigations were to prove isolated instances of fraud, the excessive and disproportionate scrutiny being placed on historically disenfranchised minority communities as a whole is likely to intimidate voters and discourage them from participating in the political process, out of fear that they will be targeted as well.

Translation: it is unsettling rather than reassuring when the Justice Department describes its mandate with bland boilerplate and glosses over the long record of abuses. For instance, the letter described a mid-1990s episode in black-majority counties in Alabama when an aggressive FBI investigation—many local voters were asked to provide samples of their signatures—yielded scant convictions for absentee ballot abuses but markedly depressed voter turnout in the next election.

Civil rights groups didn't hold out much hope for Attorney General Ashcroft, and with good reason. His spokesman Mark Corallo addressed concerns about intimidation by saying, "The only people intimidated are the people who were going to cast fraudulent ballots, and that's the point here." Of course Corallo's statement said more about the cocoon of privilege than it did about voter fraud. While FBI interviews might not deter Mr. Corallo from voting, it isn't so easy for racial and ethnic minorities to shrug it off when law enforcement shows such an intense interest.

The letter from LCCR merely put their concerns about Ashcroft's initiative on record, but the group knew better than to take the Justice Department at its word. They also used the Freedom of Information Act to demand more details about the initiative and see how, in practice, the agency balanced access and integrity.[2] For instance, what guidance were DoJ lawyers given during their annual training seminars?

It was only later in the Bush administration that the political pressures on DoJ attorneys to prosecute voter fraud cases burst into view. Republicans made a scandalous attempt to punish federal prosecutors who failed to go after alleged (or imagined) voter fraud the way the GOP wanted. It also turned out that one of the attorneys who helped lead seminars for his departmental colleagues emerged as a central figure in the scandal. And not on the side you would expect.

The Bush administration appointed David Iglesias as the U.S. attorney for New Mexico—again, the state with the narrowest margin in the 2000 election—after he had already been a JAG officer in the Navy, candidate for state attorney general, and an active supporter of the Bush campaign and other Republican candidates. Iglesias was hardly a rebel when it came to Ashcroft's initiative; he dutifully set up a special task force in New Mexico on voter fraud. What set Iglesias, and many of his fellow US attorneys, apart from Republican Party leaders was that he was a lawyer who conscientiously

followed the facts wherever they led. Much to the conster-
nation of the New Mexico GOP, the facts did not lead the
prosecutor to any indictments.

At this point we should pause briefly for a civics book
refresher on why the Department of Justice has to keep itself
scrupulously walled off from partisan politics. Because of the
department's role in our system as the law enforcement agency of last resort, it must be careful not to put a thumb on the
scale for either political party. As one precaution against in-
terfering in politics, DoJ has a longstanding practice during
campaign seasons of holding off on issuing any indictments
that would directly affect candidates in the upcoming election. So while federal laws against manipulating elections do
fall under the department's purview, it refrains from taking
action in the run-up to Election Day.

Against this backdrop, you can see how wildly inappro-
priate the below email excerpt is. It appeared in the Justice
Department Inspector General's report on their "Investigation Into the Removal of Nine U.S. Attorneys in 2006." The
email was sent five weeks before the 2004 election by former
New Mexico GOP general counsel Patrick Rogers to David
Iglesias and more than 20 other people connected with the
state Republican Party:

> I believe the [voter] ID issue should be used (now) at all
> levels – federal, state legislative races and Heather [Wil-
> son]'s race . . . . You are not going to find a better wedge
> issue . . . . I've got to believe the [voter] ID issue would
> do Heather more good than another ad talking about how
> much federal taxpayer money she has put into the (state)
> education system and social security. . . . This is the single
> best wedge issue, ever in NM. We will not have this oppor-
> tunity again…

Lest you think this was just one ill-considered email
blasted out impulsively before the NM Republicans' former

lawyer had a chance to count to ten, the Rogers email was actually part of a prolonged onslaught that resumed just before the 2006 election and included phone calls from Representative Wilson and Senator Pete Domenici personally. Then, after having been frustrated in two election cycles by U.S. Attorney Iglesias' failure to help the Republicans' capitalize on their wedge issue, the state party demanded his head on a platter. Given that similar GOP frustrations had mounted against several other federal prosecutors—in at least a few cases involving lack of action on voter fraud, but with different political grievances against other U.S. attorneys mixed in—the Bush White House was happy to oblige and lumped Iglesias into a set of a dozen dismissals. (The episode was also a landmark in the emergence of new media, as Joshua Micah Marshall's Talking Points Memo blog was instrumental in piecing together a full picture of the firings.)

Legally speaking, the administration was within its rights to replace the prosecutors. All U.S. attorneys are political appointees who serve, as the saying goes, at the pleasure of the president. The substance of the controversy was twofold. In typical fashion, the scandal was triggered by a cover-up, in this case fabricated job performance issues were used as pretexts for the firings. The other scandalous element, of course, was the fraudulent voter witch hunt—now laid bare as a partisan political gambit. As for David Iglesias, the experience left him with very clear views about voter fraud:

It's like the bogeymen parents use to scare their children. It's very frightening, and it doesn't exist. U.S. attorneys have better things to do with their time than chasing voter-fraud phantoms.

What's the Crime in That?

So who is this fraudulent voter bogeyman? Or we should instead ask, since the fraudulent voter is an imaginary figment, who do Republicans purport him or her to be? One of the most important ways to deflate this fallacy is to pinpoint the type of fraud that is claimed as the problem. In Republican-controlled state legislatures across America, lawmakers are enacting measures to keep fraudulent voters from tilting elections in Democrats' favor. Exactly how do they imagine that this is being done, and does their depiction really home in on the biggest threat to the integrity of our elections? Republicans and Democrats offer conflicting accounts of the consequences of the new laws and whether their main effect is to prevent fraudulent voting or make it harder for qualified voters to vote. Focusing on the different ways of stealing an election makes it pretty clear who is right.

The consistent thrust of the Republican voting integrity agenda is to ensure that every individual casts just one vote in their own name and does not use different personae to stuff the ballot box. Most of us are familiar with the old urban political machines' call for their constituents to 'vote early and often,' and that is the form of fraud against which the voter ID laws are aimed.

Among all the steps in the process by which votes are cast and tallied, the laws introduce restrictions at one particular point. Whenever anyone goes to a polling place to vote—as opposed to putting an absentee ballot in an envelope—they have to stop at the check-in tables before the poll workers let them go ahead and vote. The recent laws basically regulate that check-in process more tightly by imposing new requirements for proof of the voter's identity. To keep sight of an essential point, the laws make it harder for people to vote. In many cases it erects barriers for longtime residents of communities who have voted, without hassle, at the same polling places for years or even decades.

And while it might be fun to crack jokes about dead people voting, impersonating someone else at the polls—alive, dead, or fictional—is a really dumb way to try stealing an election. In his book on The Voting Wars, election law expert Rick Hasen of the University of California, Irvine walked through the practical difficulties, first by noting two options: either using the names of actual people or padding the voter rolls with made-up characters. Under the first strategy, a fraudulent voter takes a big risk of getting caught and prosecuted—particularly if the real person has already voted, or a poll worker knows what that other person looks like (or looked like, if deceased). For any political operation picking the second strategy of using fake names, it entails a lot of extra and dubiously effective effort. Not only must you mobilize your accomplices to vote, you also have to make sure they take the added step of signing up before the registration deadline. In sum, says Hasen:

> Either gambit requires assembling enough coconspirators to affect the outcome of the election. Could I do it, even in a very small election without getting caught? We don't have a single recent example of anyone even attempting it. Why try such a risky scheme when absentee ballots are so much safer and more reliable?[3]

With absentee ballots, the election burglar has more chance to supervise the process and confirm that the vote will go to the desired candidate(s). That is harder to do with the secret ballots cast at the polling place. All of these points help explain a couple of refrains that appear frequently in the literature. There is a recurring caveat in the description of instances of election chicanery: "none of which would have been prevented by the voter ID law." Conversely, whenever voter fraud alarmists present their catalogs of offenses, it's a good bet that their clearest cases involve absentee ballots rather than in-person voting.

One more note about those phony registrations. As mentioned above, Republicans use a lot of cynical humor in the voter ID debate. Sometimes the jokes serve to shut down discussion despite being way off-point. For instance Republicans have a great time LOLing about voter registration forms filled out with names like Mickey Mouse or Donald Duck. (Another cheating Democrat heard from, tee hee hee.) Seriously, do the giggling Republicans really think cartoon character names would be used as part of an effort to manipulate an election? Do they think poll workers actually would let Mickey or Donald vote? This is another example of how asymmetric polarization degrades the discourse. With lazy assumptions about the equivalence of the two political sides, the arguments aren't given enough scrutiny to keep the debate reality-based.

Republicans would have us believe this is a debate about electoral cheating. Yet they have mounted a nationwide legislative push against a form of cheating that literally no one engages in. As noted earlier, the administration of elections is a process comprised of many steps, and the GOP has made a dubious choice about where to put their focus. If we are truly looking for the perpetrators of this type of crime, we should be looking at an entirely different set of potential suspects. To stick with the crime fighting parlance, we need to ask which suspects have not just the motive, but also the opportunity. Lorraine Minnite of Rutgers University, the leading authority on electoral fraud, made the key point about this category error:

> Individual voters on their own are not capable of stealing elections, whereas election, party, and campaign officials are in a position to rig or manipulate electoral outcomes by virtue of their organizational capacity and their access to the machinery of the electoral process, two resources voters do not have.[4]

With such a disconnect between the spotlight put on individual voters as opposed to the political and governmental insiders who really do fit the profile, the instances of violations haven't lived up to the hype. Far from being orchestrators of stolen elections, the offenders in these cases made simple and understandable mistakes. Those caught voting multiple times were mostly people who went to the polls on Election Day because they worried their absentee ballot wouldn't be counted. The instances of people voting under others' names have usually been married people who thought they could vote as their spouses' proxies.

Many of the cases that have been prosecuted have been against people who cast ballots in their own names but weren't qualified to vote. In 2007 the *New York Times* published an update on the Ashcroft voting integrity crackdown that highlighted the gap between the purported threat and meager results.[5] Many of the cases centered on Milwaukee, where Republicans from other parts of Wisconsin made bold claims about election-rigging (that darn dog whistle again). Unfortunately for Kimberly Prude, Milwaukee's local U.S. attorney was more like John Ashcroft than David Iglesias. Ms. Prude was on probation in 2004 when she registered and voted, unaware it was illegal for her to do so. For at least one federal appellate judge, the prosecutor seemed overzealous. In a hearing on the case, U.S. Court of Appeals Judge Diane P. Wood said "I find this whole prosecution mysterious. I don't know whether the Eastern District of Wisconsin goes after every felon who accidentally votes."

See You in Court

One of the main battlefronts of the voter fraud debate has been the judicial review of all those voter ID laws. The pivotal question about the laws is the same one highlighted by the civil rights groups back in 2002: do they actually help combat fraud, or is their real purpose to reduce voter turnout? State and federal courts have had to weigh the legislatures' claimed need for the voting regulations (aka "state interest") against the burden it places on voters.

Compared with the floor speeches or media interviews of politicians, judicial opinions require their authors to build and support their arguments carefully. It is all the more striking, therefore, when jurists have twisted themselves into pretzels to justify the voter ID requirements. The prime examples are the 2008 Supreme Court decision in *William Crawford v. Marion County Election Board* (on Indiana's law) and the ruling of a Seventh District Court of Appeals three-judge panel in 2014 in *Ruthelle Frank v. Governor Scott Walker*.

Former Justice John Paul Stevens' majority opinion in the former case includes a section on the threat of voter fraud in Indiana is positively schizophrenic. It opens with frank acknowledgements that the voter ID law only helps combat voter impersonation, that there is no evidence of such fraud ever taking place in Indiana, and that harsh penalties protect the state against any future threat. In the next sentences, the countervailing justifications offered by Stevens were laughable. Elsewhere in the country, he notes, examples have been documented by historians (Tammany Hall-era New York is cited in the footnote), and "occasional examples have surfaced in recent years." As recently as 2003, Indiana had its own brush with voter fraud in a primary for the Mayor's race in East Chicago (though again, that was different form of fraud not addressed by Indiana's law). Those latter points, according to the high court's majority, "demonstrate that not only is the risk of voter fraud real but that it could affect the outcome of a close election."

On the other side of the scale, defenders of the ID laws have downplayed the burden they place on voters. In the Supreme Court's decision on Indiana, it said that requiring someone to pull together documents proving their identity, making a trip to the DMV, and posing for a picture "surely does not qualify as a substantial burden on the right to vote." Sure, in the experience and socio-economic circles of appellate judges, such requirements probably aren't very burdensome. But minimizing the burden shows a major disconnect with the lives of those most affected and harmed by these laws. Defenders of the laws never seriously consider the circumstances of fellow Americans who do not have drivers' licenses or other standard ID. Oblivious about the social distance separating them from the people whose access to the ballot box they're deciding, they make glib assumptions and show little sign of genuine curiosity about them.

Close observers of the judiciary like Sherrilyn Ifill and Benjamin Barton have raised concerns about the ways such blind spots can skew the law.[6] They argue that having judges with more diverse professional experience—and thus greater exposure to ground-level realities for different issues—is as important as racial and ethnic diversity, if not more. The Supreme Court's infamous *Citizens United* decision that opened the floodgates for money in politics was emblematic. After Justice Sandra Day O'Connor retired from the Court, it no longer had any members who had served in elected office. Justice O'Connor had always taken pride in her earlier political career in the Arizona state legislature, where she was senate majority leader, and she was aghast at the naivety of the *Citizens United* money-as-speech decision.

Returning to the naivety of the judges who have bolstered the voter ID laws, below is a passage from the Seventh Circuit panel opinion that upheld the Wisconsin statute. The panel majority were echoing a lower court judge's disbelief that there could be significant number of ID-less Americans…

> …in a world in which photo ID is essential to board an airplane, enter Canada or any other foreign nation, drive

a car (even people who do not own cars need licenses to drive friends' or relatives' cars), buy a beer, purchase pseudoephedrine for a stuffy nose or pickup a prescription at a pharmacy, open a bank account or cash a check at a currency exchange, buy a gun, or enter a courthouse to serve as a juror or watch the argument of this appeal.

Set aside the fact that photo ID is not required for many of the activities listed, including airline flight or the purchase of alcohol or prescription medication. Focus instead on the privileged presumptions of this account of modern life. Exchanging international currency, seriously? Plus, the author of the *Frank v. Walker* opinion apparently had difficulty conceiving of anyone who never drives (well surely they borrow friends' cars).

Even if you stop to consider basic practicalities, there are clear differences between the hassle entailed in voting versus going to the DMV. First, there are a lot more polling places than DMV offices. Unless you live right next to the DMV, chances are that your polling place is much more convenient. Second, on Election Day the polls are open from early-morning until early- or mid-evening to give voters a chance to cast their ballots before or after the work day. When judges and others shrug off a trip to the DMV as trivial, they are showing their own ignorance. Such trips are a lot more costly for an hourly wage-earner with an inflexible schedule than for your average judge.

In fact, one researcher tallied the costs incurred by nine citizens in three different states when they sought state-issued photo IDs that were ostensibly free of charge.[7] Even though Mississippi, Pennsylvania, and Texas offered the IDs without charging a fee, the subjects of the study still bore costs for transportation, time off from their jobs, and/or fees for other documents that totaled between $79-172 to obtain them (not counting the pro bono legal assistance some of them were able to access). For people with low incomes, such costs would be difficult to fit into their household budgets. Nor should they have to, in order to exercise their basic right as citizens. As the report points out, these costs far exceed the inflation-adjusted $11 price tag of the poll tax that was declared unconstitutional a half century ago at the end of the Jim Crow Era. Bear in mind, too, that these were success stories in which the IDs were indeed obtained. Others have found the hurdles—to obtain necessary documents like birth certificates, for instance—to be insurmountable.

After the Seventh Circuit panel upheld the Wisconsin law, Judge Richard Posner pressed his colleagues to vote on whether the full court should reconsider the case. The vote failed on a 5-5 tie, and the losing side signed a dissent written by Judge Posner, who is a widely respected conservative thought leader and has the distinction of being cited in the legal literature more frequently than any other scholar in America. Responding to the panel's assessment of whether Wisconsinites who lack ID are truly committed to voting, Judge Posner offered this rebuttal:

> The panel opinion notes that 22 percent of eligible voters in Wisconsin don't register to vote, and infers from this— since registration is not burdensome (you don't need to present a photo ID in order to register)—that the 22 percent simply aren't interested in voting. Fair enough. But the panel further infers that the 9 percent of registered voters who don't have photo IDs must likewise be uninterested in voting, since they are unwilling to go to the trouble of getting a photo ID. Wrong. The correct inference from the fact that registered voters lack photo IDs is the opposite of the panel's assertion that their failure to vote proves them to be uninterested in voting. Why would they have bothered to register if they didn't want to vote? Something must have happened to deter them from obtaining the photo ID that they would need in order to be permitted to vote: the in-

convenience, for some registered voters the great difficulty, of obtaining a photo ID.

Indeed, why should voters have to jump through extra hoops to demonstrate their interest in voting? In discussions on voting rights, there tends to be wide agreement that in a democratic republic they are "preservative of other basic civil and political rights." That idea somehow got lost in the Court of Appeals ruling. The way the court tipped in favor of dubious state interests is hard to square with the notion of voter enfranchisement as a bedrock principle.

In the Indiana case, for instance, much concern was focused on that state's bloated rolls of registered voters, which apparently included high numbers of people who have died or relocated. Theoretically this made Indiana elections vulnerable to voter fraud if people tried to impersonate those who have deceased or moved away. That is a mighty big *if*, however. Aside from the extreme rarity of voter impersonation, don't forget that an invalid registration is at least one step away from the kind of cheating that would affect an election outcome. The problem only arises when someone actually votes in other people's names. Which they never do.

In a dissenting opinion in *Crawford v. Marion County*, former Justice David Souter saw several difficulties with the attempt to justify the Indiana law on these grounds. For one thing, he wondered what was stopping the State of Indiana from cleaning up its voter rolls. Given that the federal government had sued the state years earlier over its failure to update the records, Souter this as proof that the state's interest wasn't so compelling after all. Justice Souter also noted that the clean-up itself could help clarify whether any voter impersonation fraud had taken place; once the state determined when an individual had died or moved, they could look to see whether any votes were cast under that name subsequently. Most important though, he questioned why bad recordkeeping on the part of the state justifies burdening the voter. As he said, "the answer to the problem is in the State's own hands." Souter went on to flag the same issue in connection with the state interest in public confidence in the electoral process. To the extent that the outdated records sparked public worry over the integrity of elections, then the answer isn't voter ID but updating the records.

Right in My Backyard

Wisconsin's voter ID law was in full effect for the first time in 2016. And it so happened that the state's annual spring election in April was also the first time my own name would appear on a ballot—as a candidate for a seat on the Stevens Point City Council. So I listened attentively when a staff expert came from the Government Accountability Board (GAB) several months before the election to give a presentation on the new law's requirements. The GAB is a key piece of Wisconsin's proud tradition of good government, but recently Gov. Walker and the Republican-controlled legislature have enacted a number of measures to clip its wings.

Listening to the GAB presentation that night, I was particularly interested in what the voter ID law would mean for students. My city council district includes a corner of one of the campuses in the University of Wisconsin system, so there are hundreds of students living in the district. While the Texas voter ID law famously allows the use of gun licenses but not student ID, the Wisconsin legislature merely set stricter limits on student ID expiration dates that rendered many of them invalid. Even though the reason was obvious, I couldn't resist asking the GAB expert why there were different rules for student ID and drivers' licenses. For the record, she resisted taking the bait and said her role was confined to explaining the legislative results rather than political or policy rationales.

I confronted a straightforward task too: prevent the new requirements from thwarting student voters. The solution was a special mailing to the student apartment complexes down the street from me. That mailer was also one of the biggest expenses of my campaign and comprised one-quarter of our budget. Because of the mismatch between standard UW-Stevens Point student IDs and the new law, many students had to get a special ID from a campus office before going to vote. As you can see from the below mailer, we appealed to the students on the grounds of not letting Governor Walker disenfranchise them. It is hard to know precisely what support I earned from students, but luckily for me, on Election Day I managed to outpoll my rightward-leaning opponent by a 16 percent margin.

You probably heard that Gov. Scott Walker and the legislature have forced students to jump through an extra hoop in the hopes it will deter you form voting. Let's prove them wrong. On April 5th you will need a photo ID to vote. Types of ID's that comply with the new law include:

- Wisconsin DOT issued ID or receipt
- Military ID
- US Passport
- Certificate of Naturalization
- Tribal ID

If you do not have an appropriate ID you are able to get one that complies with the new law through the point card office.

STEP ONE: Go to office number 340 in the DUC and ask for the Voter ID point card.

STEP TWO: On April 5 go to your local polling place 2442 Michigan Ave at the Department of Park on Recreation across the parking lot from PJ Jacobs Junior High School.

For
Shorr
Stevens Point City Council
2509 Peck Street
Stevens Point, WI 54481

Even though many students on college campuses across the state were kept waiting to vote for periods of hours (with some of them giving up and not voting), their hassles were hardly the worst of it. It took Dennis Hatten, a 53-year old African-American military veteran, six months to obtain a voter ID after moving from Illinois to get healthcare from the Milwaukee VA hospital. One problem Hatten ran into was that the name originally entered on his Arkansas birth certificate (when he got hold of it) by a Creole midwife was D'Nette rather than Dennis. Only when it was determined that Hatten's original Social Security enrollment was under the same Francophonized first name did the Wisconsin DMV accept his proof of identity. Otherwise, they insisted he would need to get the Social Security Administration (SSA) to change their records. And by the way, Hatten pushed through all this red tape with help from a local group, VoteRiders, that provided legal assistance every step of the way. Reflecting on the ordeal, he told *The Nation* that he had never had any problems voting in all his years in Illinois and commented to *ThinkProgress*, "I thought, is this sort of a poll tax type of thing? Are they trying to stop us from voting? It seemed to me like some of the veiled racist systems from the past are still in place."[8] Just as this book was going to press, the question ricocheted between the U.S. District Court in Milwaukee—which ruled that Wisconsin would have to accommodate voters who lack an ID by giving them the option of signing an affidavit—and a Seventh Circuit Court of Appeals concerned about the affidavit option being too open-ended.

Taking a step back from the legal wrangling over the Wisconsin law, the Kafkaesque experiences of Dennis Hatten and many others like him raise much broader issues. Election law expert Rick Hasen has highlighted a legal doctrine called the Democracy Canon that says for any conflicting interpretations of a statute, preference should be given to the one that enables a voter to cast their vote.[9] That is all well and good for resolving matters of law, but Hatten's experience reveals a more systemic problem that tilts things against the voter. As a matter of common sense, there is no earthly reason for a DMV official to doubt or reject the explanation that Dennis Hatten was indeed D'Nette in his first hours of life. Did the official really think Dennis was somehow fraudulently using D'Nette's birth records from 53 years earlier? In other words, voter ID laws have turned too many DMVs, city clerks' offices, secretaries of state, and election judges into skeptical gatekeepers who use the smallest discrepancies to hinder ballot access. Again, the entire process now seems contrary to the notion of voting rights as preservative of our civil and political rights.

Meanwhile as the Seventh Circuit Court of Appeals revisited *Frank v. Walker* right after the April 2016 Wisconsin spring election, they got caught between the two realms of law and administration. The court stuck to its earlier position that an ordinary trip to the DMV didn't constitute an excessive burden, but the horror stories that emerged forced the court to admit that certain obstacles can result in an "inability to obtain a qualifying photo ID with reasonable effort." Individuals facing those kinds of hurdles would now be exempt from the voter ID requirement. To prevent more cases like Mr. Hatten's, the Seventh Circuit specified that an inability to acquire ID could stem from mismatched names on birth certificates or getting hamstrung between the demands of two agencies like the DMV and SSA. The lower District Court meanwhile has mandated seemingly wider resort to affidavits as alternative to IDs, though the Court of Appeals has been resistant. But as I say, should it really take federal court rulings to deal with these types of situations? Seeing all the relatively low-level state and local officials with the power to block access to the ballot box, perhaps we need another Democracy Canon for their decisions. As in the Dennis / D'Nette Hatten case, sometimes the peculiar discrepancies and situations—odd as they might seem—are more plausible than the sinister view of someone as a fraudulent voter.

For that matter, the point can be extended to question the need for registered voters to prove their identity. Before the current round of state laws, the default assumption at the local polling place was that people were who they said they were—that checking in at the desk, signing the book, and the deterrent of severe penalties was enough to keep people honest. There wasn't a problem that needed fixing. Unless, of course, the object of the laws was to create new problems.

Correlation Equals Correlation

The major trend for the regulation of elections is clear: more states around the country are bingeing on rules and limits that put tighter constraints on voting. In effect, the legislators and governors are imposing elaborate restrictions on the citizens for whom they ostensibly work. The added irony, of course, is that all of these politicians are affiliated with the party that decries government interference in people's lives.

The Republicans' political gains in statehouses in 2010 and subsequently have truly opened the voting suppression floodgates. As Wendy Weiser of NYU's Brennan Center for Justice has pointed out, legislatures under Republican control were responsible for 18 of the 22 new sets of restrictions.[10] There were also notable relationships between the voting laws and recent demographic and political trends in the states. The Brennan Center found that laws were passed in seven of the 11 states with the highest black turnout in 2008 and also in nine of the 12 states that saw the biggest spike in their Hispanic population in the 2010 census.

Even more revealing has been the dramatic shift in another area of election administration: early voting and the chance to cast a ballot before Election Day. Until recently early voting was popular, and even many conservative states were expanding its availability. And then there was a change in who was voting early. "Just as early voting has become successful among minorities and lower-income voters," Weiser noted, "it has become a target. Since 2011 [up to 2014], eight states that saw recent increases in minority early voting usage have sharply cut back on early voting hours and days." Most famously, a number of states eliminated voting on the Sunday before Election Day, which many black churches were using to get 'souls to the polls' after Sunday services. Naturally the cutbacks in early voting forced more people to vote on Election Day, which was the main cause for the long lines at polling places in Florida in 2012. As with students in Wisconsin last spring, many Florida voters missed their chance to vote because they couldn't remain in line for so many hours—exactly the outcome that the authors of the restrictions sought.

For Judge Richard Posner, these correlations between political interests and the enactment of tighter voting regulations lay at the heart of the matter. Passages in two different sections of his dissent in *Frank v. Walker*, worth quoting at length, approach the issue from this angle:

> There is only one motivation for imposing burdens on voting that are ostensibly designed to discourage voter impersonation fraud, if there is no actual danger of such fraud, and that is to discourage voting by persons likely to vote against the party responsible for imposing the burdens.
>
> ...
>
> The data imply that a number of conservative states try to make it difficult for people who are outside the mainstream, whether because of poverty or race or problems with the English language, or who are unlikely to have a driver's license or feel comfortable dealing with officialdom, to vote, and that liberal states try to make it easy for such people to vote because if they do vote they are likely to vote for Democratic candidates. Were matters as simple as this there would no compelling reason for judicial intervention; it would be politics as usual. But actually there's an asymmetry. There is evidence both that voter impersonation fraud is extremely rare and that photo ID requirements for voting, especially of the strict variety found in Wisconsin, are likely to discourage voting. This implies that the net effect of such requirements is to impede voting

by people easily discouraged from voting, most of whom probably lean Democratic.

The first passage essentially applies Occam's Razor; if the voter fraud cover story is revealed as lacking any basis, then the opportunity for partisan advantage must be the actual objective. The second paragraph highlights important socio-economic realities and paints an apt portrait the voter ID laws' victims / targets. The people burdened by the laws' requirements are all economically marginalized. They have difficulty navigating government offices and do not view the bureaucracy as inclined to help them, particularly as the government puts new hurdles in their way. And they are the most easily deterred from making the effort—which, as Posner points out, is the nefarious purpose of the laws.

In a flurry of decisions striking down state election laws, several federal courts in summer 2016 finally waved aside all pretense about their racially discriminatory purpose. This time the judges called bullshit on the voter fraud cover story and called out state legislators for their attempts to suppress black, Hispanic, and Native American turnout. In the above mentioned case of *One Wisconsin vs. Judge Nichol*, U.S. District Judge James Peterson found that "restricting hours for in-person absentee voting, intentionally discriminates on the basis of race. I reach this conclusion because I am persuaded that this law was specifically targeted to curtail voting in Milwaukee without any other legitimate purpose." In Gov. McCrory's North Carolina, the legislative history of the restrictions actually showed the lawmakers' discriminatory intent. As U.S. Court of Appeals Judge Diana Gribbon Motz wrote, "the State's very justification for a challenged statute hinges explicitly on race -- specifically its concern that African Americans, who had overwhelmingly voted for Democrats, had too much access to the franchise."

How Far Have Republicans Fallen?

Voter ID laws are merely the latest battle in a much longer struggle over voting rights. For the last half-century, of course, that struggle has focused principally on the enfranchisement of African-Americans, and the main instrument for protecting their rights was the 1965 Voting Rights Act (VRA). To trace the trajectory of the Republican Party on these issues, it is instructive to look at Republicans' posture toward the Voting Rights Act—particularly the judicial and legislative battles over law's application and its periodic reauthorization by Congress. A review of that record shows a contentious internal fight between the GOP's moderate and hard-right wings. Until, that is, the current decade when movement conservatives decisively gained the upper hand.

In America's national mythology, the civil rights movement and reforms of the mid-20th Century demonstrated our country's capacity for justice and self-renewal. We tell ourselves a story of triumph over hate and prejudice. Rosa Parks and Martin Luther King are the iconic heroes in that story, and Representative John Lewis, survivor of Bloody Sunday on Selma Alabama's Edmund Pettus Bridge is a living legend. To the extent those successes are proud legacies of the nation as a whole, then by definition they should transcend partisan politics. Unfortunately the recent hollowing out of the VRA puts that into question. The 2016 presidential election will be the first in which states with clear histories of voting rights violations have emerged from being under federal supervision. This development was brought about by right wing Republicans eager to declare problem solved on racism in America. They have shown the same out-of-touchness that was discussed earlier—a tendency to push abstract principles rather than extend themselves to understand realities beyond their personal experience. And one of their most influential champions is now the chief justice of the U.S. Supreme Court.

The GOP's rightward shift on voting rights can be plotted across three rounds of fighting over the VRA: in 1982, 2006, and in connection with a 2013 Supreme Court decision that removed one of the Act's core provisions. In the early 1980s, debate focused on the legal threshold for determining election rules to be discriminatory. Was it necessary to show that the electoral game was purposely rigged against a minority group, or could discrimination be inferred even when there isn't a detailed blueprint for racial oppression? A common tactic for diluting the power of a community's black populace was to elect all of its council members on an at-large basis instead of dividing up the map into districts. Just because the result was lily white city councils and county boards, many conservatives didn't view that outcome as proof of discrimination. As they saw it, the protection of voting rights should only clear the path to the ballot, not necessarily to seats of political power. Through the 1970s, the VRA was used to reform local electoral systems that, in effect, blocked blacks from being elected to office.

Then in their 1980 decision on *Mobile v. Bolden*, the Supreme Court affirmed the conservative view of the post-Civil War Fifteenth Amendment:

> The Amendment does not entail the right to have Negro candidates elected, but prohibits only purposefully discriminatory denial or abridgment by government of the freedom to vote "on account of race, color, or previous condition of servitude."

The Court's decision shifted the action to Congress, which in 1982 crafted an extension of the VRA. The Democratic-controlled House of Representatives kicked off by adopting a version that would revert to the previous standard of proof—

that discrimination could be discerned from the effects of an electoral system, without needing the smoking gun of discriminatory intent. When leaders in the Republican-controlled Senate put up resistance, spurred on by the Reagan administration Justice Department, the extension seemed headed for a deadlock. The stalemate was broken when Senator Bob Dole offered a compromise largely in line with the House version. Dole argued that Republicans should make "the extra effort to erase the lingering image of our party as the cadre of the elite, the wealthy, the insensitive…Our job now is to demonstrate concern to blacks and others who doubt our sincerity."[11] His proposal ultimately passed in the Senate by a margin of 85-8.

Among the Republicans in the House who helped shepherd the 1982 VRA renewal was Rep. Jim Sensenbrenner of Wisconsin (yes, the same Rep. Sensenbrenner). By the mid-2000s Sensenbrenner was chair of the House Judiciary Committee and bent on passing the next reauthorization in 2006. Even though it had been four decades since the VRA was adopted, Sensenbrenner still saw a clear need for the law to keep discriminatory practices in check. When they launched their effort, the bill's cosponsors named it after civil rights icons Fannie Lou Hamer, Coretta Scott King, and Rosa Parks.

The fight in 2006 centered on Section 5 of the VRA, which required that any proposed election rule changes in states with histories of discrimination be cleared at the federal level by the Justice Department. Not surprisingly the states chafed under the so-called preclearance requirement, and the right wing insisted it was no longer necessary as the Jim Crow era receded into the past. But don't try telling that to the lawyers at the Justice Department; in the 24 years since the last reauthorization, they had rejected over 500 proposed changes in states covered by Section 5. The bipartisan consensus on voting rights held firm in 2006. Not only did the House pass the Hamer-King-Parks bill by an overwhelming bipartisan majority of 390-33, it was adopted unanimously in the Senate (98-0).

The protagonist in the next act of the VRA drama was, like Sensenbrenner, a Republican who had worked behind the scenes in the early-1980s and meanwhile risen to an influential position. Early in his career, Supreme Court Chief Justice John Roberts was a special assistant to Reagan administration Attorney General William French Smith. During the 1982 reauthorization battle, Roberts was extremely active, circulating a raft of internal memos, preparing administration officials' congressional testimony, and coordinating with sympathetic congressmembers—all aimed at fending off the "effects test" for judging discriminatory electoral measures from their results rather than intentions.[12]

At his 2005 Senate confirmation hearing to be chief justice, Roberts offered a small 'C' conservative philosophy that limited the Court's role to building on legal precedent rather than making major changes to the law. That view was hard to square with his actions eight years later in the matter of *Shelby County v. Holder*, which swept aside the express will of Congress in their reauthorization of the Voting Rights Act. In specific, the Court declared it unconstitutional that states were subjected to Article 5 preclearance for their past misdeeds (the justices must not have heard about the more recent misdeeds that failed preclearance). There were glimpses during the *Shelby County* oral arguments of 80s-vintage DoJ staffer John Roberts—as distinct from chief justice nominee John Roberts, with his talk of "calling balls and strikes." As Ari Berman highlights, Roberts made a big show during oral arguments of the surprisingly high ranking of Massachusetts when it comes to racial disparities in voter registration. He was trying to show that by 2013 the realities of race in America had changed more than people realized. But the changes were less than Roberts realized; his facts about Massachusetts were totally wrong.[13] In terms of controversial statements that day, however, Roberts couldn't hold a candle to late-Justice Antonin Scalia who talked about the protections of the Voting Rights Act as a form of "racial entitlement" and drew audible gasps in the Court chamber.

Just as it had 30 years earlier, the Court effectively served the ball back into Congress' court. And while Congressman Sensenbrenner's personal commitment to preserving the VRA is unflagging, he has become an almost solitary figure within his House Republican caucus as bipartisan efforts have completely broken down. In 2014 Sensenbrenner spearheaded the Voting Rights Amendment Act, with the support of senior figures in his party such as then-House Majority Leader Eric Cantor. For Democrats, the price for bipartisanship and the chance to get something passed was a bill that left out the recent spate of voter ID laws. Then after the bipartisan bill stalled in the House, and Eric Cantor was defeated by a primary opponent, Democrats fashioned a much stronger bill. As the ranking Democrat on the Senate Judiciary Committee, Patrick Leahy, told *The Nation*'s Ari Berman, "We made compromises to get [Republican] support and they didn't keep their word. So this time I decided to listen to the voters who had their right to vote blocked, and they asked for strong legislation that fully restores the protections of the VRA."[14] This has been one of the consistent patterns of asymmetric polarization: Democrats go the extra mile for compromise and get nothing in return.

A Revised Election Integrity Agenda

In his victory speech on the night of the 2012 election, President Obama thanked everyone who turned out, "whether you voted for the very first time or waited in line for a very long time." Then the president added "by the way, we have to fix that." On that November Tuesday, an estimated five million Americans had to wait more than an hour to vote. Yet with the responsibility for governing and running elections spread across 50 states and approximately 8,000 local jurisdictions, fixing the wait times and other election system weaknesses is a complex task.

In order to at least clarify some of the problems and solutions, the Obama and Romney campaigns' top election law attorneys joined forces to lead the Presidential Commission on Election Administration. The Commission issued its findings in February 2014, and if you combine them with similar expert studies, an agenda emerges on which Republicans and Democrats may be able to cooperate. As with the three fallacies covered in the other chapters, though, a healthier debate will only be possible with a significant shift of stance by Republicans.

The key thing is to straighten out the working assumptions about the threat to election integrity. It doesn't take a constitutional scholar to see how the burdens placed on voters and the interests claimed by the state have gotten out of whack. You don't have to be David Souter to spot the absurdity of the State of Indiana imposing an ID requirement on voters on the grounds of the sloppy condition of the State's own registration records. Republican state legislatures have put up barriers between voters and the ballot box based on a combination of imaginary fraud and more plausible threats that would not even be affected by the new restrictions.

And so Topic A in a rebooted election policy debate is the lifting of draconian voter ID requirements in favor of a common sense approach to confirming voters' identities. Making ID free of charge or even opening DMV offices for longer hours is merely window dressing—a chance for states to try appearing reasonable while still leaving an onerous burden on the voter. As Myrna Pérez of the Brennan Center points out "There are ways to meet integrity concerns without disenfranchising eligible citizens." She highlights Louisiana, Michigan, and Rhode Island, which use a combination of signed affidavits, checking against the voter rolls, and provisional ballots.[15] The rules for provisional ballots should tilt toward their being counted, as is the case in Rhode Island. In too many states, provisional ballots constitute another hoop voters have to jump through, often with the end result that their votes are not counted.

Pérez also discusses ways to shift the onus for registration and the maintenance of up-to-date voter rolls from the voter to the government by making them automatic, electronic, and/or online. Under automatic registration it falls to the state to register its citizens to vote, linking its drivers' license system—among others—to the voter rolls. Such connections between agencies can be used not only to enroll voters (with an opt-out for those who'd prefer not), but to update voter records when an agency becomes aware of someone moving to a new address. These systems would be electronic, a shift away from paper records similar to the digitization of medical records. They also cut down on a major source of errors in voter rolls: mis-transcriptions of information from handwritten forms. California and Oregon have been at the leading edge of automatic registration. And finally, online registration gives voters the ability to sign up at their nearest terminal, a system being put in place in over 30 states.[16]

For its part, the Presidential Commission also put a high priority on early voting. In many states, reduced days for early voting led to the long polling place lines that prompted the commission to be set up. Noting that almost one in three voters had already cast their ballots by Election Day 2012 (double the proportion from 12 years earlier), the commission viewed early voting as a necessity:

> Whatever the form and design of in-person or mail voting in any one state, the trend toward increasing the time period for voting is certain to continue. Stated simply, early voting offers Americans opportunities to participate in the

electoral process that simply cannot be afforded by the contained twelve-hour period of the traditional Election Day. Election officials from both parties testified to the importance of early voting in alleviating the congestion and other potential problems of a single Election Day.

They also stressed a concern about voting equipment all around the country reaching the end of its lifecycle and pointed out the hurdles impeding the next generation of technology from coming on the market. Election laws in many states require voting machines to meet federal standards, yet those standards are nearly as archaic as the machines themselves. The guidelines that technical experts developed for the next generation of equipment ran into delays in the relevant federal standard-setting body: the U.S. Election Assistance Commission. That group has been such a beleaguered political punching bag that it's had trouble recruiting members to serve on it. As the 2013-2014 presidential panel and others have emphasized, the technology gap also makes it that much more important for local election officials to put their machines through rigorous testing and audit election results thoroughly.

As a final agenda item on the revised election integrity agenda, the same rigor and vigilance should be applied to the officials involved in the machinery of elections as to the hardware itself. Remembering Lorraine Minnite's earlier point, it is those with direct access to the behind-the-scenes process—rather than individual voters—who are in a position to commit fraud. In that same spirit, the Brennan Center's Myrna Pérez says the proper aim of fraud prevention is to "protect against insider wrongdoing," for which she borrows lessons from the private sector. In other words, election officials need systems very similar to the kind of financial controls that organizations use to prevent the misappropriation of funds. Registrations, voting machines, ballots, and result tallies should all be handled in accordance with responsibilities assigned to the appropriate personnel, robust internal checks, and suitable security measures. Experience in the private sector has also shown the importance of anonymous tip lines to help ensure fraud is reported and public exposure of confirmed fraud to make sure it's deterred.[17]

As is the case with all four fallacies, any shift to a policy debate that is more middle-of-the-road and pragmatic would ask a lot of Republicans. It would require them to heed former Wisconsin State Senator Dale Schultz's call for campaigns of ideas and reject Paul Weyrich's strategy of trying to limit the size of the electorate. Of course there are serious problems with the Republicans' ideas, but when it comes to the mechanics of conducting elections, Sen. Schultz's plea at least has the virtue of upholding our country's democratic principles.

Further Reading

Berman, Ari. *Give Us the Ballot: The Modern Struggle for Voting Rights in America.* New York: Farar, Straus and Giroux, 2015.

Hasen, Richard L. *The Voting Wars: From Florida 2000 to the Next Election Meltdown.* New Haven: Yale University Press, 2012.

Minnite, Lorraine C. *The Myth of Voter Fraud.* Ithaca: Cornell University Press, 2010.

Waldman, Michael. *The RFight to Vote.* New York: Simon & Schuster, 2016.

6

The Problem With Republican Ideas

Speaker of the House Paul Ryan is an apt spokesman at a disheartening moment for our political system, but not in the way he intends. Ryan has always seen himself as his party's high-minded leader and substantive thinker. His election-year series of "Better Way" working papers followed his usual mode of issuing the kind of reports more typical of an institute than a legislative office. And they strike a none-too-subtle contrast with his party's presidential nominee, whose campaign has been remarkable for its lack of position papers, or a policy operation, or even any vaguely plausible proposals. Speaker Ryan happily provides the wonkish counterpoint to Donald Trump's ignorant bluster. As the Speaker drove the point home in his speech to the 2016 Republican National Convention in Cleveland, he is well rooted in the GOP's philosophy and principles:

> Yet we know better than to think that Republicans can
> win only on the failures of Democrats. It still comes down

to the contest of ideas. Which is really good news, ladies and gentlemen, because when it's about ideas, the advantage goes to us.

Against the dreary backdrop of arrogant bureaucracies, pointless mandates, reckless borrowing, willful retreat in the world, and all that progressives still have in store for us, the Republican Party stands as the great, enduring alternative.

We believe in making government, as Ronald Reagan said, not the distributor of gifts and privilege, but once again the protector of our liberties.

Let the other party go on making its case for more government control over every aspect of our lives—more taxes to pay, more debt to carry, more rules to follow, more judges who just make it up as they go along.

Yet Ryan is only substantive in relative comparison to Trump, which is setting the bar very low. With the benefit of having read this book, you can probably spot the superficiality and distortion in Ryan's convention speech—the attack on the social safety net, hyping of a deficit that has actually been shrinking, the denigration of government. From his "distributor of gifts" rhetoric, it's clear that the Speaker didn't get Arthur Brooks' memo about libertarian stereotypes and making peace with the safety net.

What makes Paul Ryan an apt symbol of our dysfunctional discourse, though, is the absurdity of casting a staunch far-right figure as the would-be rescuer of the Republican Party. Speaker Ryan typifies the impractical policy approaches that flow from the right wing's vacuous ideas. Ryan's working papers are just as fanciful as his Ayn Rand-inspired rhetoric. The ideas about consumer-driven healthcare on which he based his Obamacare alternative have been thoroughly debunked.[1]

Tellingly, Speaker Ryan's record of legislative accomplishments after 18 years in office is paper-thin. According to a study by University of Wisconsin political scientist David T. Canon, Ryan's congressional resume includes just three bills adopted into law, including the naming of a post office and a change in the taxation of deer-hunting. The *New York Times* cited the study as well as other scholars in a July 2016 assessment of Ryan. The *Times* report quoted Professor Canon explaining that, "Paul Ryan is not a detail kind of legislator in terms of putting bills together to pass." George Washington University's Sarah Binder was quoted making a similar point:

> "He has tried to burnish his political brand as the carrier of a conservative, ideological torch. That reputation would come crashing down very quickly if he actually had to write and negotiate a bill with trade-offs, compromises, 'pay-fors,' etc. That would open up fissures within his G.O.P. conference, let alone with Democrats who could filibuster in the Senate."[2]

Where Prof. Canon sees a certain work style and Prof. Binder a clash between personal branding and political forces, I see an ideological orthodoxy that is cut off from the practical realities of governing. This is more than just a problem of one politician's approach to legislating. Contrary to what Paul Ryan told the party faithful in Cleveland, when it's about ideas, Republicans are at a distinct disadvantage. Their ideas simply do not square with how the world really works, and as a result their prescriptions are unworkable. Healthcare consumer purchasing power cannot get consumers a better deal, only government regulation can. The private sector can't pull the economy out of a deep recession.

The four major policy fallacies show how movement conservative ideology has led the Republican Party astray and undermined its ability to govern. The GOP has become wedded to ideas that put up barriers against pragmatism. The fallacy of beneficent job creators is the veneration of a group, business owners, with a vastly inflated sense of their role in the economy. If Republicans had their way during the Great Recession—with the government had stepping back and letting the private sector heal itself—Alan Blinder and Mark Zandi estimated that the economy in 2015 would have had 3.6 million fewer jobs and an unemployment rate of 7.6 percent rather than 5.0 percent.[3] The facts of high corporate profit levels and the mounting wealth of the top one percent contradict the notion of beleaguered job creators. And given the difficulties confronting wage earners struggling to get by, the growing income gap also refutes the idea that job creators' successes are the key to prosperity for the rest of us.

On healthcare, Republicans have gotten wrapped up in a libertarian pet theory. A laissez-faire approach to healthcare is so wildly unrealistic it is hard to imagine how it's supposed to work. Are we supposed to wait for appendectomies to go on special, or scan our newspaper circulars for coupons? Should we look on eBay for the best deal on angioplasty? According to the GOP's theory, we consumers just need empowerment to squeeze the physicians, hospitals, and insurance companies for better deals. But as Republicans have tried cherry picking the 'good parts' of Obamacare, they've been trapped in a huge contradiction. Despite all the free market rhetoric about getting government off the backs of the private sector, the good parts of Obamacare are regulations on the insurance industry. The free market will not keep adult children on their parents' insurance until age 26, or cap consumers' out of pocket costs, extend coverage to 20 million uninsured Americans, or guarantee coverage of preexisting conditions. As a matter of fact, it was the insurance industry's failure to do those things that gave rise to the Affordable Care Act.

The foreign policy fallacy of an almighty America is a delusion of grandeur and control. Republicans seem no longer able to distinguish between arrogance and leadership. They presume America's moral authority instead of being good stewards of American exceptionalism. It makes one wonder how Republican politicians handle their own positions of leadership and authority. It probably wouldn't work very well in their communities to bark orders and throw their weight around, and that type of brutishness doesn't work any better in the international arena.

While Republicans try painting Democrats as ambivalent about American power, they are trying to shift focus away from the real partisan divide. The right wing's delusions of U.S. omnipotence make them utterly ham-handed in the exercise of American power and leadership. The prevailing Democratic foreign policy approach works from an understanding that the United States cannot achieve its international aims without the goodwill and support of others. One of the most unsettling things after the Bush administration's invasion of Iraq was the loss of legitimacy and sympathy around the world. As mentioned earlier, it was precisely because many serious-minded Republican foreign policy specialists were worried about U.S. global standing that they took part in our 2007 *Bridging the Foreign Policy Divide* book project.

I also noted that those particular specialists are no longer the main spokespersons of Republican foreign policy. And when their successors talk about building coalitions or partnerships, today's GOP message shows no appreciation for the diligent back-and-forth required to gain international support. Instead we mostly hear vague rhetoric about standing-to-shoulder with allies. That is why Republicans were so wildly unrealistic about getting a better nuclear deal with Iran, especially the further sanctions that would've been needed. Recall that Senate Minority Leader Dick Durbin brought in ambassadors from the key countries so senators could hear the message that the deal that'd been negotiated was the best available, and there would be no tightening of sanctions.

One of the juicy ironies of our dysfunctional politics is the idea that liberals are naïve and conservatives are more realistic. Yet the Republicans' fallacies on the economy, healthcare, and foreign policy show them to be extremely naïve. One of the core concepts of classic conservatism is pessimism about human nature, and yet the deregulatory agenda of today's movement conservatives tries to remove all checks and constraints on the behavior of business owners. What did they think would happen when you remove the disincentives for coal companies to spew toxic pollutants? And what leads Republicans to believe that 'empowered consumers' can get a better bargain for themselves than insurance regulations? Then on foreign policy, the GOP approach to national security is rife with barstool bluster. On the challenges of both Iran and the Islamic State, they have put more focus on highlighting our adversaries' well-known brutality than on practical responses. To paraphrase Mayor Giuliani, using the words "radical Islamic terrorism" and calling for its defeat—or for the hell to be knocked out of it—is not a strategy.

On voting rights, the barrier Republicans put between themselves and reality is a cover story of imagined misdeeds—tinged with political and racial prejudice. Think of Congressman Grothman's fundamental belief about Democratic Party cheating and all the references in those debates to places like inner-city Milwaukee and St. Louis. Perhaps Rep. Grothman's belief is genuine, but other Americans are coming to recognize that it lacks any basis in fact. As this book was going to press, the country's judiciary was finally demanding changes to Republican voter ID laws. The courts' reassessment of the laws seems like a hopeful sign of the political system's capacity for self-correction. The truth might win out after all—just the tonic we need in order to address asymmetric polarization.

But because of the stakes and lack of supporting facts, it is important to ask how the voter fraud fraud was so successful in the first place. Prof. Lorraine Minnite offers a compelling explanation for why it is still possible to disenfranchise citizens long after the reforms of the 1960s-1980s:

> Administrative complexities justified as race-neutral necessities for deterring voter fraud are also opportunities for administrative error that have come to replace opportunities for vote suppression by other means. This is the context for the proliferation of unsupported fraud allegations today. The allegations shrewdly veil a political strategy for winning elections by tamping down turnout among socially subordinate groups. It is the most vulnerable voters, those with the least education or the least experience in operating the machinery of the electoral process, that are most in need of the simplest rules and the easiest access. Thus, it is these voters who stand in for the criminal voters conjured up by spurious voter fraud allegations and imagined by the U.S. cultural myth of voter fraud.[4]

So it is no accident that low-level clerks and poll workers have been turned into hyper-vigilant gatekeepers of ballot access. The very purpose of the Republican strategy has been to hang a cloud of suspicion over the voting process and convince the low-level administrators that the complex rules are needed to catch cheaters. It has taken this long for the rules to start being scrutinized and checked to see whether they meet a valid need. To the extent that this represents a failure of the judiciary, we should remember Sherrilyn Ifill and Benjamin Barton's point about the need for judges with enough range of experience to spot ill-founded arguments (think Sandra Day O'Connor and *Citizens United*).

The myth-building about fraudulent voters and mucking around with election rules are much bigger threats to voting integrity than the specter of voter fraud that Republicans raise. The political party that stood to benefit from the new laws couched them as modest protections. The voter ID laws were sold partly on the premise that almost everyone has the required forms of identification—a premise accepted at face value by too many judges. How were so many voter ID requirements adopted before crucial facts were recognized? While the laws' backers couldn't imagine modern life without a state-issued ID, roughly 10 percent of their fellow citizens were indeed living without them (and an even higher proportion of minorities). And as Profs. Minnite and Hasen have highlighted, the suppressive effect goes beyond people who lack ID. Merely by creating the aura of criminality, Republicans can deter many who are at society's margins from voting even if they have the required ID.

Asymmetric polarization is the natural consequence of one political party's sustained lurch to the political extreme. Unfortunately that party has suffered very few consequences for its radicalism—a classic moral hazard problem. In the American body politic, we have yet to reckon with the market failure in our marketplace of ideas. The point of the four fallacies is that Republicans haven't been forced to come up with new material, even as they have drifted into self-parody and left themselves little basis to govern pragmatically. Let's revisit then-White House Chief of Staff Rahm Emanuel's comment on the drafting of the Affordable Care Act:

> This will be bipartisan; there will be ideas from both parties and individuals from both parties in the final product. Whether Republicans decide to vote for things they promoted will be up to them.

By now we should recognize that bipartisanship cannot be a virtue for its own sake. We cannot have a productive policy discourse without judging the merits and practicality of a party's positions on an issue. Rahm Emanuel was right, by 2009 congressional Democrats had already incorporated ideas into the ACA that used to be considered conservative.

Why should Democrats have to chase Republicans when the latter have wandered off into substantive incoherence?

The ball is squarely in the Republicans' court. As I was working on this project a fellow Democrat asked about our party's need for self-reflection. No doubt there are issues with which Democrats need to wrestle. But those are not the urgent issues of this moment in our history, and Democrats will not do our party or our country any favors by looking inward. In fact, the four fallacies and other far-right misconceptions have shrunk the political space for us to push center-left ideas. If we want to have public options included in the health insurance exchanges, then we have to puncture the image of Obamacare as unpopular. Note also that the attempt to compromise with Republicans on voting rights required that voter ID laws be excluded from the deal. Calling bullshit on the Republicans is a first-order precondition for yanking the country's political center of gravity and national conversation back toward the middle.

And we have seen how even well-intentioned moderate conservatives make hasty calls for bipartisanship before their party makes an honest effort to adjust course. How can the American Enterprise Institute's Arthur Brooks claim the GOP appreciates the need for public goods and isn't as libertarian as people think? His comment in the Georgetown University exchange with President Obama is a sign of how much conservative self-examination is still needed. In other words, a reform-minded thought leader is trying to claim credit for the GOP's supposed moderation without there being any sign of it in the statements of party leaders or their policy positions.

Perhaps Donald Trump represents the American political system hitting bottom, in terms of the GOP's rightward drift. Republicans needed to see ugly nativism and fascist flirtations to recognize what the Tea Party hath wrought— the exact John Birch-style extremism that earlier generations of conservatives forcefully resisted. The horror and resistance aroused by Trump offers some reassurance in the fact that the nation hasn't lost our ability to be shocked.

But the emergence of House Speaker Paul Ryan as the anti-Trump highlights another problem: the way our senses had already grown dull by the time Trump came along. Yes, Trump's appeal to intolerance and white America's sense of grievance is especially repugnant. We need to take a close look, however, at Speaker Ryan's sunnier alternative and not be so quick to accept it as an answer to America's challenges. I have been looking for Arthur Brooks' non-libertarian Republicans and would celebrate any effort to pull their party back toward the center. All I've seen so far is congressmembers willing to keep the federal government from shutting down and a few governors who accept Medicaid expansion and veto the worst forms of homophobic discrimination. These things do not constitute a moderate GOP in the making.

So I will keep waiting for a meaningful shift in the Republicans' approach—one that refocuses on real problems and solutions. That would mean, for instance, stopping demonizing teachers or offering vouchers and charter schools as miracle cures or ignoring the massive imbalances in school system resources (and family resources) that have re-segregated education in America. Until then, it is incumbent on all of us to call bullshit.

Notes

Chapter 1

1. Thomas E. Mann and Norman J. Ornstein, "Let's just say it: The Republicans are the problem," *Washington Post*, April 27, 2012.

Chapter 2

1. Mitch McConnell, "Focus Must Be on Job Creators," *Politico*, September 7, 2011.
2. Jim Sensenbrenner, "Obamacare Has Been a Disaster," *Stevens Point Journal* and other *USA Today* network newspapers in Wisconsin, May 13, 2016.
3. David Shorr, "GOP Slanderously Misrepresents Obamacare," *Stevens Point Journal*, May 20, 2016.
4. John Paul Rollert, "Make Way (Again) for the 'Job Creators,'" Roosevelt Institute, September 28, 2011.
5. Nicholas J. Hanauer, "Raise Taxes on Rich to Reward True Job Creators," Bloomberg View, November 30, 2011.
6. Jim Houser, "Small Businesses Need Customers, Not

Tax Cuts for the Wealthy," Oregon Center for Public Policy, November 2010.

7. Thomas E. Mann and Norman J. Ornstein, *It's Even Worse Than It ~~Looks~~ Was,* (New York: Perseus Books, 2016), p. 119.

8. Alan S. Blinder and Mark Zandi, "The Financial Crisis: Lessons for the Next One," Center on Budget and Policy Priorities, October 15, 2015.

9. Michael Grunwald, *The New New Deal,* (New York: Simon and Schuster, 2012), p. 338.David Corn, *Showdown,* (New York: William Morrow, 2012).

10. Mackenzie Weinger, "Poll Exclusive: Obama Winning Message War," *The Politico,* October 3, 2012.

11. Richard Whisnant, "N.C. Environmental Legislation, 2015: Deregulating and obscuring the consequences," Environmental Law in Context blog, University of North Carolina School of Government, October 28, 2015.

12. Dan Kaufman, "Scott Walker and the Fate of the Union," The New York Times Magazine, June 12, 2015.

13. Ann Markusen, "The High Road Wins: How and Why Minnesota is Outpacing Wisconsin," *The American Prospect,* May 8, 2015.

14. Lauren Windsor, "Caught on Tape: What Mitch McConnell Complained About to a Roomful of Billionaires," *The Nation,* August 26, 2014.

15. Jacob S. Hacker and Paul Pierson, *American Amnesia: How the War on Government Led Us To Forget What Made America Prosper,* (New York: Simon & Schuster, 2016), p. 142.

16. Bryce Covert, "Top Conservative: 'We Have to Declare Peace on the Safety Net,'" *Think Progress,* October 30, 2013.

17. Michael R. Strain, "A Jobs Agenda for the Right," *National Affairs,* Winter 2014, p. 6.

18. EJ Dionne, "The Reformicons," *Democracy*, Summer 2014.

19. Arthur Brooks, "Be Open-Handed Toward Your Brothers," *Commentary*, February 1, 2014

20. Marguerite Roza, Chris Lozier, and Cristina Sepe, "K–12 Job Trends Amidst Stimulus Funds: Early Findings," Schools in Crisis: Making Ends Meet, May 2010.

Chapter 3

1. Atul Gawande, "The Cost Conundrum," *The New Yorker*, June 1, 2009.

2. Jonathan Chait, "The Lonely Death of the Republican Health Care Plan," *New York*, February 6, 2014.

3. John McDonough and Max Fletcher, "What Would Republicans Do Instead of the Affordable Care Act?," Health Affairs Blog, September 18, 2015. For chart see: https://jemcd1.files.wordpress.com/2015/09/gop-conservative-aca-replacement-proposals-comparison.pdf

4. Paul Star, *Remedy and Reaction: The Peculiar American Struggle Over Health Care Reform*, (New Haven: Yale University Press, 2013), p. 52.

5. The text of the Kristol memo was posted by Josh Marshall on his Talking Points Memo blog at: http://talkingpointsmemo.com/edblog/the-1993-kristol-memo-on-defeating-health-care-reform

6. Starr, pp. 122-123.

7. Sarah Kliff, "This is why Obamacare is canceling some people's insurance plans," Washington Post Wonkblog, October 29, 2013.

8. Cf. Gawande, "The Cost Conundrum."

9. Jay Hancock "An Obamacare Payment Reform Success Story – One Health System, Two Procedures," Kaiser Health News, April 30, 2015.

10. Barack Obama, "United States Health Care Reform: Progress to Date and Next Steps," *Journal of the Ameri-*

can *Medical Association*, July 11, 2016.

11. Ezekiel J. Emanuel, *Reinventing American Healthcare*, (New York: Public Affairs Books, 2014), p. 123.

12. Dana Milbank, "Washington Sketch: At Breakfast With Emanuel, a Side of Sausage-Making," *Washington Post*, June 26, 2009.

Chapter 4

1. Derek Chollet, Tod Lindberg, and David Shorr (eds.), *Bridging the Foreign Policy Divide*, (New York: Routledge, 2008).

2. "Transcript: Donald Trump on NATO, Turkey's Coup Attempt, and the World," *The New York Times*, July 21, 2016.

3. Marco Rubio, "Restoring America's Strength," *Foreign Affairs*, September/October 2015.

4. Tom Vanden Brook, "Attack on Iran could set back bomb effort two years," *USA Today*, August 23, 2015.

5. Derek Chollet, *The Long Game: How Obama Defied Washington and Redefined America's Role in the World*, (New York: Public Affairs Books, 2016), p. 133.

6. Greg Jaffe, "Hope fades on Obama's vow to bring troops home before presidency ends," *Washington Post*, October 12, 2015.

7. Chollet, p. 153 (Kindle edition).

8. David Shorr, "Think Again: Climate Treaties," *Foreign Policy*, March/April 2014.

9. Ruth Greenspan Bell and Micah S. Ziegler (eds.), "Building International Climate Cooperation: Lessons from the weapons and trade regimes for achieving international climate goals," Washington, DC: World Resources Institute, 2012.

10. Richard Fontaine, "Obama's 'Slippery Slope' Delusion," *Politico Magazine*, January 14, 2016.

Chapter 5

1. Ari Berman, *Give Us the Ballot: The Modern Struggle for Voting Rights in America*, (New York: Farar, Straus and Giroux, 2015), p. 216.
2. Lorraine Minnite, *The Myth of Voter Fraud*, (Ithaca: Cornell University Press, 2010), pp. 218-24.
3. Richard L. Hasen, *The Voting Wars: From Florida 2000 to the Next Election Meltdown*, (New Haven: Yale University Press, 2012), pp. 61-62.
4. Minnite, op. cit. p. 19.
5. Eric Lipton and Ian Urbina, "In 5-Year Effort, Scant Evidence of Voter Fraud," *New York Times*, April 12, 2007.
6. Sherrilyn Iffil, "A Court Out of Touch: Today's Justices Do Not Hear the Real America," *The Nation*, September 13, 2012 and Emily Bazelon, "How to Bring the Supreme Court Back Down to Earth," *New York Times Magazine*, February 15, 2016.
7. Richard Sobel, "The High Cost of 'Free' Photo Voter Identification Cards," Charles Hamilton Houston Institute for Race and Justice, Harvard Law School, June 2014.
8. Ari Berman, "Wisconsin's Voter ID Law Caused Major Problems at the Polls Last Night," *The Nation*, April 6, 2016 and Alice Ollstein, "Wisconsin's Voter ID Law Is Back In Court Following Election Day Woes," *ThinkProgress*, April 8, 2016.
9. Hasen, op. cit. pp. 23, 108.
10. Wendy Weiser, "Voter Suppression: How Bad? (Pretty Bad)," *The American Prospect*, Fall 2014.
11. *Give Us the Ballot*, page 155.
12. Ibid, pp. 149-152.
13. Ibid, pp. 274-276.
14. Ari Berman, "Congressional Democrats Introduce Ambitious New Bill to Restore the Voting Rights Act," *The Nation*, June 24, 2015.

15. Myrna Pérez, "Election Integrity: A Pro-Voter Agenda," Brennan Center for Justice, 2016, p. 13.
16. Ibid, pp. 4-6.
17. Ibid, pp. 16-17.

Chapter 6

1. For a comprehensive examination, see Timothy Stoltz-fus Jost, *Health Care At Risk: A Critique of the Consumer-Driven Movement,* (Durham: Duke University Press, 2007).
2. Jackie Calmes, "Paul Ryan's Worst Ally," *New York Times,* July 9, 2016.
3. Blinder and Zandi op. cit.
4. Minnite, op. cit. pp 88-89.

Index

www.ingramcontent.com/pod-product-compliance
Lightning Source LLC
Chambersburg PA
CBHW021619270326
41931CB00008B/766